SHAMANIC DRUMMING

Calling the Spirits

Michael Drake

SHAMANIC DRUMMING

The shamanic methodology presented in this book should not be viewed as a substitute for orthodox medical or psychological treatment, but should instead be considered a complementary treatment. This book is not intended as a substitute for the medical advice of physicians. The reader should regularly consult a physician in matters relating to his/her health and particularly with respect to any symptoms that may require diagnosis or medical attention. I trust you will use your own discretion and intuitive wisdom as to how shamanic drumming may be appropriate to your particular needs.

Cover Art: A Creative Commons licensed derivative of a Sámi shamanic drum contributed by Christopher Forster and Tor Gjerde.

Dedication

To master drum maker Judith Thomson—who above all, was a wise, generous, and beloved friend. Her extraordinary passion and tireless devotion to "the way of the drum" has been a wellspring of inspiration for me. She mentored many drum makers and keepers in many communities across the United States and Canada. Hers was an authentic life well lived and she will be deeply missed.

SHAMANIC DRUMMING

Contents

SHAMANIC DRUMMING

Acknowledgments

This book is the culmination of a twenty-year journey into rhythm. My quest to understand the power of rhythm has been aided by many people. Although it would be impossible to mention everyone here, I would like to express my gratitude to:

My wife Elisia, whose loving support allowed me to bring this work to fruition.

Douglas R. Ward, spiritual teacher, healer, and visionary for illuminating the path and showing me the way.

Mongolian shaman Jade Wah'oo Grigori for initiating me in the drum ways of his tradition, and for helping me to find my own path of rhythm.

Cathy Dawn Perkins for her profound vision, insight, and counsel.

Native American elders Les Thomas, Don Fasthorse, and Ed Bills for sharing the rhythms and ceremonials of their traditions.

The members of our community drum circle for sustaining a commitment to come together in rhythm for nearly twenty years.

And finally, I am especially grateful to the spirit of the drum for guiding me on my journey into rhythm.

SHAMANIC DRUMMING

Introduction

Shamanism has achieved a dramatic modern resurgence. A recent study by one of the foremost scholars on shamanism today reveals that the contemporary world still hungers for transcendent experiences because the shamanic narrative is hard-wired in us all. In his 2010 book, *Shamanism: A Biopsychosocial Paradigm of Consciousness and Healing*, Michael Winkelman presents the shamanic paradigm within a biopsychosocial framework for explaining successful human evolution through group rituals. According to Winkelman, shamanism is rooted in innate functions of the brain, mind, and consciousness. As Winkelman puts it, "The cross-cultural manifestations of basic experiences related to shamanism (e.g., soul flight, death-and-rebirth, animal identities) illustrates that these practices are not strictly cultural but are structured by underlying, biologically inherent structures. These are neurobiological structures of knowing that provide the universal aspects of the human brain/mind"[1]

The psychobiological basis of shamanism provided it with functional roles in survival and cultural evolution, producing an evolved psychology that has applications in relatively intractable modern problems such as addictions treatment and in addressing the consequences of psychological trauma, alienation, and disconnectedness. Winkelman elaborates on shamanism as a paradigm of self-empowerment, which strengthens individuals' ability to take an active role in their health and well-being. Shamanic practices produce deeper self-awareness by enhancing the use of the entire brain and provide "a vital connection with community and the spiritual dimensions of human health that have been lacking in modern societies."[2]

Furthermore, recent studies demonstrate that the innate modules of rhythm, like percussion or dance, provide a secular approach to accessing a higher power and applying spiritual perspectives. The *American Journal of Public Health* reviewed drum therapy in its April 2003 edition, concluding that "shamanic drumming directly supports the introduction of spiritual factors found significant in the healing process. Shamanic activities bring people efficiently and directly into immediate encounters with spiritual forces, focusing the client on the whole body and integrating healing at physical and spiritual levels. This process allows them to connect with the power of the universe, to externalize their own knowledge, and to internalize their answers; it also enhances their sense of empowerment and responsibility. These experiences are healing, bringing the restorative powers of nature to clinical settings."[3]

What is shamanism?

Christina Pratt, author of *An Encyclopedia of Shamanism*, defines a shaman as a practitioner who has developed the mastery of "accessing altered states of consciousness" and "mediating between the needs of the spirit world and those of the physical world in a way that can be understood by the community ...."[4] Shamanism is the intentional effort to acquire and nurture ongoing relationships with personal helping spirits by journeying into realms where the spirits dwell. The reason for developing personal relationships with spirit helpers is to gain wisdom, healing techniques, and other vital information that can benefit the community.

In shamanic healing, it is the spirit helpers who do much of the actual healing work. In some ways, it might be more accurate to call the shaman the spirit's helper rather than vice-versa. John Trehero, a Shoshone Sun Dance chief, derived his healing power from frequent dreams about the beaver. He described his spirit helper thus: "I dreamed about the beaver. The beaver said here is my power, and then he showed me his front paws. If a person has pain I feel with my hand on him, and that pain comes in my hand. I use my own hands for beaver paws."[5]

In doing their healing work, the shaman may use a variety of tools. These could include plants, stones, feathers, and musical instruments. However, it should be remembered that each of these also holds power and are spirit helpers for the shaman in their own right. It is this intimate relationship with spirit and the use of trance states that distinguishes the shaman from other practitioners.

The shaman's trance is an intentionally induced state of ecstasy. Shamanic trance is characterized by its flexibility, ranging from a light diagnostic state to spirit flight to full embodiment by spirit. Shamans use intention and discipline to control the nature, depth, and qualities of their trance states. The shaman may progress through a range of trance states until they reach the level that is necessary for healing to occur.

The capacity to enter a range of trance states is a natural manifestation of human consciousness. The ability to enter trance states makes us human, not shamans. What makes shamans unique is their mastery over an otherwise normal human trait. It requires training, practice, and devotion to master any expressive art. Shamans master the art of ecstasy to see the true nature of the universe.

Shamanism is a way of perceiving the nature of the universe in a way that incorporates the normally invisible world where the spirits of all material things dwell. Shamans have different terms and phrases for the unseen world, but most of them clearly imply that it is the realm where the spirits of the land, animals, ancestors, and other spiritual entities dwell. Spirit encompasses all the immaterial forms of life energy that surround us. We are woven together into a net of life energies that are all around us. These energies can appear to us in different forms, such as spirits of nature, animals, or ancestors. The spirit world is the web of life itself.

Shamanism represents a universal conceptual framework found among indigenous tribal humans. It includes the belief that the natural world has two aspects: ordinary everyday awareness, formed by our habitual behaviors, patterns of belief, social norms, and cultural conditioning; and a second non-ordinary awareness accessed through altered states, or trance, induced by shamanic practices such as repetitive drumming. This second-order awareness can be developed over time or appear all at once, but once it is discerned the world is never the same. According to shamanic theory, the ordinary and non-ordinary worlds interact continuously, and a shamanic practitioner can gain knowledge about how to alter ordinary reality by taking direct action in the non-ordinary aspect of the world.

In her essay "Awakening into Dreamtime: The Shaman's Journey," Wynne Hanner explores the Australian Aboriginal concept of Dreamtime as a source of and guide to transforming our own world view. According to Aboriginal mythology, Dreamtime is a sacred era in which ancestral spirit beings formed The Creation. Indigenous Australians believe the world is real only because it has been dreamed into being. Hanner explains, "The Aborigines embrace the concept of 'reality dreaming', with reality and Dreamtime intertwined. Reality can be illusion, deception, learning, perception, experience, and is the evolution of consciousness in the alchemy of time. Reality shifts and changes like the flow of the collective unconscious, and is in constant motion creating new spiral patterns of experience. Reality, in its illusion, is the dream from which we all awaken.

To understand and work with these concepts is to awaken into the dream."[6]

Shamans employ methods for altering consciousness so that they can send their souls into the non-ordinary reality of the spirits who become their friends, guides, guardians, instructors, and allies. These helping spirits might be the spirits of nature, animals, plants, the elements, ancestors, gods, goddesses, or teachers from various religious traditions. The act of sending one's soul into the spirit world is called the soul flight or shamanic journey, and it allows the journeyer to view life and life's problems from a detached, spiritual perspective not easily achieved in a state of ordinary consciousness. One of the most universal methods for altering consciousness for this spirit journey is a persistent, mesmerizing drumbeat.

The shaman's drum

The drum, sometimes called the shaman's horse, provides the shaman a relatively easy means of controlled transcendence. Researchers have found that if a drum beat frequency of around three to four beats per second is sustained for at least fifteen minutes, it will induce significant trance states in most people, even on their first attempt. During shamanic flight, the sound of the drum serves as a guidance system, indicating where the shaman is at any moment or where they might need to go. "The drumbeat also serves as an anchor, or lifeline, that the shaman follows to return to his or her body and/or exit the trance state when the trance work is complete."[7]

The sound of the shaman's drum is very important. A shamanic ritual often begins with heating the drum head over a fire to bring it up to the desired pitch. It is the subtle variations in timbre and ever-changing overtones of the drum that allow the shaman to communicate with the spiritual realm. Part of the shaman's training involves learning to hear and interpret a larger range of frequencies than the normal person can. The shaman listens and finds the right tone, the right sound to which the spirits will respond. Through the many tones, pitches, and harmonics of the drum, the shaman communes with the subtle and normally unseen energies of the spirit world.

Tuvan shamans believe that the spirits of nature create their own sound world, and it is possible for humans to communicate with them through the sound of the drum. According to Tuvan ethnographer and former shaman Mongush Kenin-Lopsan, "We understand the spirits answers mostly from the tangible results of the communication, in terms of benefit or harm. But some people actually hear the spirits singing."[8] Tuvan shamans use the drum to convey to the spirits of a place their greetings, any requests, and thanks. It is a spiritual practice designed to help human beings relate to all of nature. Tuva (southern Siberia) is one of the few places in the world where the shamanic heritage has remained unbroken.

Drumming opens the shaman's inner, spiritual ears and eyes and also calls the helping spirits. As Tuvan musicologist Valentina Suzukei explains, "By changing and listening to the frequencies and overtones of the drum, the shaman is able to send messages to, and receive them from, both the spirit world and the patient. For example, the shaman might use the overtones to send signals to the sky, where they provoke a voice from the cosmos; in turn, the cosmic signals are caught on the drum and reflected to the shaman through the creation of subsequent overtones."[9]

The shaman's universe

Shamans believe that this direct communication is possible because the entire universe exists within human consciousness. According to shamanic cosmology, there are three inner planes of consciousness: the Upper, Middle, and Lower Worlds. Humans did not invent these inner realms; they discovered them. Far from being a human contrivance, these archetypal worlds are inherent in the collective unconscious, the common psychological inheritance of humanity. They are woven into the matrix of the psyche. They are a part of our psyche, a part of us whether we choose to become aware of it or not.

The world above is the unseen realm of unmanifest potential, higher knowledge, and enlightenment. The Upper or Celestial Realm is the domain of gods, goddesses, and evolved teachers. It is in this inner realm that the archetypal patterns, which are the blueprints for all things, exist. According to Lakota shaman Nick Black Elk, "This is the real world that is behind this one, and everything we see here is something like a shadow from that world."[10] The Celestial Realm forms the matrix of possibilities that correspond to the world we experience through our mind and senses. All situations, conditions, and states of being are a manifestation of a world of archetypes. Every event in the visible world is the effect of an image or pattern in the unseen world.

Shamans journey to the Upper World to acquire archetypal knowledge, to bring a vision into being, or to influence events in the material world. By interacting with the archetypes, the shaman interacts with their counterparts in the outer world. Shamans also go there for inspiration, insight, or to find ways to restore balance in the world. As anthropologist and author Felicitas Goodman points out, "One of the most pervasive traditions of shamanic cultures is the insight that there exists a patterned cosmological order, which can be disturbed by human activity."[11] When harmony between the human realm and the original intended pattern is disturbed, the shaman makes a spirit journey to the Celestial Realm to bring back the balance.

The Middle World is the spirit counterpart of the material realm and the inner region that is most like outer reality. Nick Black Elk spoke of the realm "where there is nothing but the spirits of all things."[12] In this parallel world exist the spirits that are the essence of everything in the material world. The Middle World is so truly parallel to the world in which we live that we can journey across it and visit all the places, people, and things we know in ordinary reality. Spirit journeys in the middle world provide a means of travel and communication without cars, planes, or telephones. It is a means of exploring territory to find the location of healing herbs or game, or to establish communication links over great distances.

The Lower World is the realm of animal spirits, spirit guides, and the dead—the place to which human spirits travel upon physical death. This Lower World is not Hell as defined by the agricultural religious traditions such as Christianity. It is the place of tests and challenges, but also the realm of power where guardian animals or helping spirits are acquired. A spirit journey to the Lower World is generally undertaken to seek the help and guidance of an animal spirit, to recover lost power, or to find and return a sick person's wandering spirit.

The three realms are linked together by a vertical axis that is commonly referred to as the "World Tree." The Mongols call this axis the *turge* tree. The mythic Eagle, who was the first shaman (*buu*), perches at the top of the *turge* tree, which touches the sky by the Pole Star (*Altan Hadaas*). A tree of seven branches with a bird or eagle at the top and a serpent at the roots is symbolism often found on prehistoric monuments. The roots of the World Tree touch the Lower World. Its trunk is the Middle World, and its branches hold up the Upper World.

14

This central axis exists within each of us. Through the sound of the drum, which is invariably made of wood from the World Tree, the shaman is transported to the axis within and conveyed from plane to plane. As Tuvan musicologist Valentina Suzukei explains: "There is a bridge on these sound waves so you can go from one world to another. In the sound world, a tunnel opens through which we can pass, or the shaman's spirits come to us. When you stop playing the drum, the bridge disappears."[13] The inner axis passes through an opening or hole through which the shaman can ascend to the Celestial Realm of unmanifest potential and descend on healing journeys into the temporal realm of manifest form.

Shamans believe that the three worlds are more than interconnected: they also interact with one another. The shaman can perceive, influence, and harmonize their interactions. Through conscious articulation, the shaman brings the three realms into accord.

The key to understanding the shaman's world is to realize that the universe is made of vibrational energy: that it is a single, flowing, rhythmic being. According to quantum physics, everything in the universe, from the smallest subatomic particle to the largest star, has an inherent vibrational pattern. The entire universe is created through vibration and can be influenced through the vibrations of shamanic drumming. The shaman's drum is a tool for altering the vibrational state of the shaman and/or the patient or a particular situation in the community.

Experiencing rhythms in the body

Shamanic drum ways provide the opportunity to acquire shamanic experiences. The techniques are simple and effective. Before exploring the drum methods outlined in this book, it would be beneficial for the reader to experience how the body responds to different rhythms. Whether you drum or merely tap your fingers, learn to "feel the beat" by allowing it to sink into your body and consciousness. Notice how your body responds to each pattern. Keep in mind that the manner in which you play or shape a rhythm will affect your response. One of the paradoxes of rhythm is that it has both the capacity to move your awareness out of your body into realms beyond time and space and to ground you firmly in the present moment.

Begin by playing a steady, metronome-like rhythm with uniform time intervals. A clockwork drum beat generates a dynamic energy that is yang, creative, and expansive in nature. Dynamic energies are ascending forces that carry consciousness into higher realms. At a rapid tempo of three to four beats per second, a steady, rhythmic pattern, or "eagle-beat," will arouse and vitalize you. It creates the sensation of inner movement, which, if you allow it, will carry you along. As you continue to drum, you will become more ecstatic. You and your drum will seem to merge. You may speed up or slow down. That is perfectly normal. Shamanic trance is characterized by its range and flexibility, so don't get hung up on trying to maintain a certain speed. It can be distracting and your hands may get tired. Follow your inner sense of timing as to both tempo and duration.

After drumming the eagle-beat, simply relax and bathe in the sonic afterglow of physical and spiritual well-being. When the final drumbeat fades into silence, an inaudible, yet perceptible pulsation persists for a brief period. This silent pulse is ever-present within each of us, but our awareness is rarely in sync with it. Sense this silent pulse resonating within your body. You may experience the sensation of every particle in your body pulsing in sync with the rhythm you just played. This inner pulse entrains to the rhythmic pattern as soon as you begin to drum.

Next, try playing the steady pulse of a heartbeat rhythm. A two-beat rhythm produces a different sonic experience. The soft, steady lub-dub, lub-dub of a heartbeat rhythm has a calming and centering affect. It reconnects us to the warmth and safety of the first sound we ever heard—the nurturing pulse of our mother's heartbeat melding with our own. According to Ted Andrews, author of *Animal Speak*, "a rhythm of two is a rhythm that helps connect you to the feminine energies of creative imagination, birth, and intuition."[14] At a more rapid tempo, the heartbeat rhythm stimulates a downward flow of energy within the body. It generates a magnetic energy that is yin, intuitive, and receptive in nature. Magnetic energies are descending forces conducive to great healing, mind, and regenerative powers.

These two simple drum patterns form the rhythmic basis of this book. They are the healing rhythms I use most often in my shamanic work. Moreover, they are rhythm archetypes representing yin—the form giving principle of energy, and yang—the principle of life and consciousness immanent in all phenomena. Yin and yang are the binary elements that generate between them the totality of existence. A binary progression underlies the structure of reality. At a fundamental level, the laws of the universe are written in a binary code. The binary mathematical system forms the basis of computer languages and applies to nearly everything from crystalline structures to the genetic code. The binary basis of the genetic code is formed by the plus and minus strands of DNA.

The human experience is a microcosm and reflection of binary progression. The archetypes of rhythm are the fundamental patterns that underlie our resonant field of reality. Entraining to these archetypal rhythms, we experience them directly and discover our rhythmic interconnections. Each pattern pulsates specific qualities of energy that give inherent structure and meaning to the possibilities of being. They exist in every human being from the moment of conception to the final breath. Each human being is an integral composite of the archetypes of rhythm. Each of us is a series of rhythmic patterns summed up as a single inner pulse, the essential aspect of our being.

Becoming a shaman

Many people in today's world are being called by spirit to become shamans. A yearning exists deep within many of us to reconnect to the natural world. It is a call to a life lived in balance with awareness of nature, of spirit, and of self. We live in a culture that has severed itself from nature and spirit. Humans have lost touch with the spirit world and the wisdom of inner knowing. The spirits, however, have not forgotten us. They are calling us to a path of environmental sanity, to rejoining the miraculous cycle of nature.

The spirits call many to work with them, but only a few may respond to the call. Choosing to ignore a calling may have undesirable consequences or none at all. For some, it can lead to depression and illness as the life force is constricted and thwarted. Those who choose to follow their shamanic calling may have no idea how to begin.

What do you do if the ancestral shamanic tradition no longer exists in your culture, but you still feel the call today? While traditional, indigenous shamanism continues to decline around the world, shamanic ideology has gradually entered Western humanities and social sciences and developed into the neo-shamanic movement. Neo-shamanism is a term used to describe the creation or revival of a shamanic culture. Most modern shamanic practitioners fall into this category. Neo-shamanism is not a single, cohesive belief system, but a collective term for many such philosophies.

Neo-shamans use a variety of core techniques from different shamanic disciplines.

Mircea Eliade, a religious scholar, was perhaps the first to write about neo-shamanism. In his classic work, *Shamanism: Archaic Techniques of Ecstasy*, Eliade discusses the three stages of becoming a shaman: the Call, Training, and Initiation. The first stage to becoming a healer, as described by Eliade, is that of the calling—this call comes from the family, the community, or from the world beyond. Some are called, initiated and trained by spirit guides and/or human teachers from childhood.

Spirit calls us to a path of shamanism in many ways. It can be as dramatic as a life threatening illness or as simple as a dream. According to Mongolian shaman Sarangerel Odigon, "one of the most reliable marks of a shamanic calling is the urge to learn how to become a shaman."[15] The call functions to awaken our own inner knowing and the yearning to express our true self through the artistry of the shaman.

Shamans are called, and then receive rigorous instruction. Training may follow an ordered tradition or take a spontaneous course guided by the shaman's spirit helpers. The function of training is to develop the skills and talents so that shamanic practitioners don't unintentionally hurt themselves or others. Though the spirits give shamans their healing powers, shamans must learn the technique of invoking them. Traditional shamanic training requires considerable devotion and personal sacrifice, not so much to gain power, but to become the person who can wield that power responsibly. Ongoing practice and learning are essential to perfecting any art or skill.

Where does one find shamanic training in the digital age? There are growing numbers of spiritual seekers who learn about shamanism from the internet or through reading the published works of individuals who have received shamanic training. Though a handbook is no substitute for an apprenticeship program, it can convey the fundamental methodological information. Authentic shamanic knowledge can only be acquired through individual experience; however, one must first acquire the methods in order to utilize them. Once you have learned the basic skills, your helping spirits can provide you all the training you need.

Then there is Initiation. Shamanic initiation is a rite of passage, connecting the apprentice shaman intimately to the spirit world. It is typically the final step in shamanic training, though initiation may be set in motion at any time by spirit's intervention into the initiate's life. Ultimately, shamanic initiation takes place between the initiate and the spirit world. It is the spirits who choose and make the shaman.

This book recounts my own journey into shamanic practice and explores what someone should do if they feel the call to become a shaman. Working with the guidance of my helping spirits, I have written a guide to becoming a shamanic healer that encompasses the power of the drum, of community, and of the accountability inherent in authentic shamanic practice.

How does someone embark on the shamanic path? To be an effective shamanic healer, one must go through the three steps. The first step is to acknowledge the calling.

SHAMANIC DRUMMING

Chapter 1

The Calling

Follow your bliss and the universe will open doors where there were only walls.
—Joseph Campbell

Though the subtitle of this book is *Calling the Spirits*, it was the spirits who first called me to a path of shamanism. I do not know why I was chosen. I ceased making such queries long ago. Over the years, I learned to just go with the flow. The how and why of my circumstances became less important to me than the lessons that I was learning along the way. As time passed, I began to see how my life experiences honed me into the artist I am today.

For as long as I can remember, I have been an explorer—pushing beyond familiar territory to investigate the unknown. As a child, I had a near-drowning, out-of-body experience that opened my eyes to the hidden dimensions of life and propelled my explorations. Like everyone, I was trying to find myself. I was also searching for something that resonated with me—anything that evoked a shared emotion or belief. I identified with people whose words were congruent with their actions. My inner self was most nourished when I was immersed in nature. Being introverted and eccentric, I often felt a closer kinship to nature than I did to people.

My birthplace was Oklahoma, but Topeka, Kansas became my home at the age of five until I moved away at age twenty-three. I was raised in a conservative Southern Baptist Church, which shaped my personal ethics and early life. I had my first ecstatic experience as a youth at a church revival, an evangelistic meeting intended to reawaken interest in religion. This state of rapture and trancelike elation inspired my spiritual quest. For much of my youth, I had aspirations of attending seminary to prepare for some form of ministry. I met my wife, Elisia, at a church function. We were wed by our pastor in a church wedding in 1976.

As a child, I had a voracious appetite for books. My mother took me often to the neighborhood bookmobile to find new stories. I loved a good story. I still do. I grew up in a family of articulate storytellers. Listening to my elders tell stories at family reunions was captivating entertainment. They could spin engaging yarns or recount humorous anecdotes.

There was also music at the family reunions in Oklahoma. My relatives referred to these large musical gatherings as hootenannies. Musicians and singers performed folk, gospel, country, and bluegrass often with the audience joining in. Instruments included guitar, fiddle, mandolin, banjo, blues harp, accordion, washboard, and so on. The music often started in the afternoon and continued late into the night. I savored every melodic moment.

Music and storytelling strongly influenced my artistic inclinations. Though I had aspirations of becoming a musician, my greatest talent turned out to be writing. Being shy and introverted, writing became a way to fully express myself. In high school, my English teachers supported and encouraged my creative writing. By the time I graduated in 1972, I had decided to forgo seminary and pursue a career in journalism instead. Unfortunately, my parents could not afford to send me to Kansas University, the nearest college offering a degree in journalism. To save money, I chose business as a major at Washburn University in my home town. I could live at home and work nights to pay my way. Though business was my major, I savored literature and composition courses, along with electives like sociology, anthropology, and philosophy.

After I graduated from college in 1977, I felt a great pull to "Go West." I mailed résumés to employers up and down the Pacific Coast. As fate would have it, I was offered a job with the Glidden Paint Company in Portland, Oregon. Elisia and I promptly sold our house and moved to Oregon. As a couple, that is how we often did things and that is how we still do things, after thirty-five years of marriage. We decide to do something, and then we just do it. Elisia and I have learned to trust and follow our inner yearnings. One of the things we learned working with spirits is that they often prompt us, through urges, to do one thing or another.

Upon our arrival in Portland, we soon found a house to rent. After settling in, we spent most of our free time hiking and exploring. Enamored with my new home, I began studying the geology and ecology of the

Pacific Northwest. What I began to understand is that nature sustains us and everything around us through an interdependent web of life. There is no separateness. We are all one consciousness.

I like the way George Leonard describes our vibrational connections in his book *The Silent Pulse*: "Each human being consists of pure information expressed as rhythmic waves that start as infinitesimal vibrations of subatomic particles and build outward as ever-widening resonant hierarchies of atoms, molecules, cells, organs, organisms, families, bands, tribes, nations, civilizations, and beyond."[1] At every phase of unfoldment, every entity is interwoven through the resonant web of information that is the universe.

This holistic awareness stirred a longing deep within me to reconnect to the natural world. I spent as much time as possible outdoors. I hiked, camped, backpacked and climbed volcanic peaks throughout the Northwest. Henry David Thoreau, John Muir, Aldo Leopold, Rachel Carson and Edward Abbey were my literary influences at that time in my life. In his classic book *Desert Solitaire*, Edward Abbey summed up my feelings about nature in one sentence: "But the love of wilderness is more than a hunger for what is always beyond reach; it is also an expression of loyalty to the earth, the earth which bore us and sustains us, the only home we shall ever know, the only paradise we ever need—if only we had the eyes to see."[2]

The journey

In early 1980, I lost my retail managerial job. I was ready for a change and, with so much free time, I took up reading full-time. One of the influential books that I read was *The Dharma Bums*, a 1958 novel by Beat Generation author Jack Kerouac. Kerouac's semi-fictional accounts of hiking and hitchhiking through the West inspired me to embark, with my wife's blessing, on a backpacking/gold prospecting adventure to northern California. After all, in 1980 the price of gold hit a then-record of $873 an ounce.

In May of 1980, my journey began with a bus ride to Yreka, California. From Yreka, I planned to hike and hitch my way about fifty-three miles over a mountain pass to Sawyers Bar, California. I stepped off the bus in Yreka, shouldered my heavy pack, and started walking south on State Route 3. After walking a few miles, a local farrier in a pickup offered me a ride to the small town of Etna. I spent an uneventful night camped in the Etna City Park.

On day two, I arose early and continued my trek. After a few hours of steep climbing, I hitched another ride with a traveling salesman in a station wagon to the Etna-Salmon Mountain Summit (elevation: 5,958 feet). I camped along the Pacific Crest Trail near the summit, overlooking the Salmon Mountains of Klamath National Forest about sixty miles northeast of Eureka, California. I was alone on a remote mountain pass. It was pure ecstasy.

When I awoke on the third morning of my journey, I discovered fresh cougar tracks just outside my tent. At that moment, I realized just how "in the wild" I truly was. I broke camp and continued on, hitching another ride to Idlewild Campground, a forest service recreation area on the North Fork Salmon River six miles from Sawyers Bar, California. Idlewild became my base camp for prospecting and further explorations in the surrounding area.

After a few days of unsuccessful gold-panning, I decided to backpack into nearby Marble Mountain Wilderness. I walked up Mule Bridge Road along the scenic North Fork Salmon River until I reached the wilderness trailhead. From the trailhead, I hiked the North Fork Trail deep into Marble Mountain Wilderness.

I met no one along the trail. I was alone in the wilderness. Late in the afternoon, I came upon the skeletal remains of large bear along the trail. It was one of the most peculiar sights that have I ever beheld. The skeletal paws of the bear resembled human hands and the massive skull was quite intimidating. I later learned that a local bear hunter had reportedly shot a dangerous nuisance bear, but had not killed it outright. The wounded bear had then escaped, but eventually died next to the trail.

I dropped my pack and walked a short distance down the trail to a river crossing. The North Fork Salmon River was swollen with spring snow melt, making it unsafe to cross. It began to drizzle again; it had been raining off and on all day. I had no choice but to turn around and look for a suitable place to camp for the night. Wouldn't you know it; the only level campsite was only a short distance from the bear skeleton.

I certainly was in bear country. There were tracks in the sand and mud all along the riverbank. I came across a bear footprint so large that I could step into it with my size 12 Vibram-soled boots. It wasn't a fresh track, but it was at the base of an ancient cedar in the very grove of trees where I was going to have to camp for the night. All of the large cedar trees in the area bore the claw marks of a bear marking its territory. The claw marks were so high on the tree trunks that I could barely touch them with my fingertips when standing on the tips of my toes. This was a very large bear and I was going to have to spend the night in its territory in a dark grove of trees along a raging river. I took some comfort in the fact that the tracks and markings might have been made by the bear that I discovered along the trail before it died.

I was nervous to say the least. I am always on my guard when trekking through bear country. After setting up my tent, I fired up my camp stove and cooked a hot meal. To minimize odors that might attract bears, I hung my nylon food bag from a high tree limb some distance away from the camp. I then gathered up as much firewood as I could find for the long night ahead. I found some cedar bark, which is useful for getting a camp-fire started under soggy conditions. Once the fire was going, I stacked damp wood around the perimeter of the fire pit so that it would slowly dry. Heat from the flames warmed my face and hands and the warm glow perked up my spirits. As long as the fire burned, I felt relatively safe. I tended the flames late into the night until I finally ran out of wood.

Without the comfort of a warming fire, I had no choice but to crawl into my tent and try and get some sleep. I lay awake in my sleeping bag for a long time, listening to the night sounds. I focused intently on every strange noise I heard outside my tent. To get to sleep, I focused my attention on the current rushing over the river rocks. At times, the river made haunting sounds as it rolled big rocks along its course. At some point, I fell into a deep sleep.

Then it started; the most terrifying experience of my life. I was awakened by a mysterious roar. It resembled the sound of a helicopter hovering directly over my tent. The previous day, before entering the wilderness, I had heard the "whop-whop-whop" sound of a dual-rotor logging helicopter in the distance. Helicopters, like all motorized vehicles, are prohibited in designated wilderness areas. Rationally, I knew it was highly unlikely that the sound was emanating from a helicopter hovering over my tent, yet a whirling windlike howl filled my ears in the predawn darkness. I have never been so frightened in all my life. I had spent countless nights, camping in wilderness areas across the West and never had I experienced anything like *this*.

As I opened my eyes, I realized that I couldn't move, or I was too afraid to move. I was virtually paralyzed. I lay rigid inside my sleeping bag and prayed that whatever was outside my tent would just go away. My heart pounded like a drum. My panicked mind was reeling, as I struggled to classify what I was experiencing. Frenzied thoughts of UFOs, alien abductions, and even Sasquatch raced through my mind. I don't know how long the mind-bending experience lasted. It was all so surreal. I started to hyperventilate. Death seemed imminent.

Suddenly, the eerie moaning stopped and the bizarre incident ceased, almost as abruptly as it had begun. I could hear the roaring river again, along with the pitter-patter of rain drops bouncing off the top of my nylon tent.

The paralysis ended immediately and I gasped in a lungful of air. I finally managed to sit up in my sleeping bag, my body trembling in shock. I sat motionless, lost in my thoughts, wondering what had just happened to me. The entire experience was much too real to have been a nightmare. As I relived the terrifying event in my mind again and again, the first light of dawn illuminated my tent.

I arose, hastily packed my gear, and then marched out of there as fast as I could. I retreated from the wilderness, returning to Idlewild Campground—back to familiar territory. Upon my arrival on May 18th, (1980) I learned from a fellow camper that Mt. St. Helens had erupted earlier that day at 8:32 a.m., killing fifty-seven people. The destructive power and devastation of the eruption served to distract me from my disturbing pre-dawn experience. Though I prefer the isolation and quietude of the wilderness, I spent the remaining two weeks of my vacation camped in this developed campground, never venturing back into Marble Mountain Wilderness.

During my stay in this idyllic area, I made many new friends. I met mountain climbers, backpackers, gold prospectors, miners, kayakers, a hermit, and a colorful assortment of local hippies living on gold mining claims and growing weed. All in all, it was an epic adventure for me. I will never forget it. Idlewild Campground became a restful sanctuary for me at that moment in time. Where the North Fork Salmon River wrapped around my camp, the soothing sound of the water lulled me into a peaceful sleep every night.

Chapter 2

The Initiation

One thing that comes out in myths is that at the bottom of the abyss comes the voice of salvation. The black moment is the moment when the real message of transformation is going to come. At the darkest moment comes the light.
—Joseph Campbell

Many years later I began to understand the significance of my anomalous Marble Mountain experience, although I realize that I will never understand it fully. I have come to accept that there will always be that which is unknown to me—that which is "the Great Mystery."

I now also know that the eerie howl that aroused me on that fateful night resembled that of a bullroarer. A bullroarer is a thin, feather-shaped piece of wood that, when whirled in the air by means of an attached string, makes a loud humming or roaring sound. Bullroarers produce a range of infrasonics, extremely low frequency sound waves that are picked up by the cochlea (labyrinth) of the ear, stimulating a wide array of euphoric trance states. The bullroarer dates back to the Stone Age, and is probably the most widespread among all sacred instruments. With over sixty names, it is universally linked to thunder and spirit beings in the sky.

These roaring sticks are used in certain ceremonial dances in the Desert Southwest to invoke wind and rain. In some areas of the world, the instrument played a role in certain rites of passage. The sound of the bullroarer's spiral-shaped movement is widely considered to be the voice of an ancestor, a spirit, or a deity.

The first time I actually heard a bullroarer was in December of 1991. Elisia and I were traveling through New Mexico on a cross-country tour, promoting my newly released book, *The Shamanic Drum*. By chance we happened upon the annual Shalako festival, which is a series of dances and ceremonies conducted by the Zuni people near the winter solstice in which they celebrate the return of the sun and pray for rain, growth, and fertility. Shalako is named for its masked dancers who embody kachinas or ancestral spirits. Kachinas mediate between humanity and the gods of rain and prosperity in a sacred ritual performance that ensures the transformation of winter's death into spring's rebirth. Standing ten-feet tall and resembling birds, the colorful Shalako kachinas dance rhythmically, clacking their long beaks together. They come to the human realm to collect the people's prayers and take them back to the spirit realm.

On the day of the Shalako ceremony, the six kachinas, one for each of the four cardinal directions plus zenith and nadir, entered Zuni Pueblo at dusk. Each Shalako deity was escorted by a group of singers and an attendant whirling a bullroarer over his head. As the first procession filed into the plaza, the sound of the bullroarer elicited an intense feeling of déjà vu, triggering memories of my traumatic experience in Marble Mountain Wilderness. Reflecting on my ordeal created anew the conditions for revelation, learning, and reintegration. I finally realized what had transpired on that life-altering night in 1980. Although I didn't know it back then, my guardian or tutelary spirit was "calling" me. Chosen by the spirit of a bear, my shamanic initiation had begun and, like a sluggish bear emerging from the slumber of winter hibernation, I gradually awakened to the knowing of my true self.

Shamanic initiation

Shamanic initiation is a rite of passage connecting the apprentice shaman intimately to spirit. It is probably the most powerful and least understood of all forms of spiritual awakening. It is not achieved by having mastered a body of knowledge or having completed some long-term training program. Though it may be set in motion by an apprentice's human teachers as part of an ordered, training process, authentic initiation can only be conveyed by the spirits themselves.

Shamanic initiation takes place between you and spirit, and you will know it when it happens. My own initiation came early in the timeline of my shamanic experience. It is typically the final step in becoming a shamanic healer, facilitated by the aspirant's shamanic teachers as part of a training program. However, initiation may also be spontaneous, triggered by spirit's intervention into the initiate's life. To be initiated by a helping spirit forever transforms your life. For the uninitiated, this can be problematic, to say the least. They may have no clear idea of what is happening to them, and may find themselves overwhelmed by fear of their non-ordinary experience.

I have since had other initiation experiences, such as a shamanic death-and-rebirth. However, none of these subsequent experiences have impacted me as much as my Marble Mountain experience did in 1980. That mystical encounter with spirit shattered my ego, cracking me wide open. Shamanic initiation serves as a transformer—it causes a radical change in the initiate forever. An initiation marks a transition into a new way of being in the world. It tells us something about the mystery of life and death.

According to shamanic teacher and author Sandra Ingerman, "Initiation is the death, dismembering, and dissolving of old forms/structures/ways of life. And I have come to understand that true initiation is allowing spirit to sing into creation the new forms and new creations. Allowing spirit to sing formlessness into form creates a new evolution of consciousness."[1]

Global dismemberment

So very many are asking the same question these days: "What is happening around us?" We see severe climate change, massive oil spills, and species dying off. We see corruption in banking, politics, and religions around the world. We see fear, anger, and hopelessness in our communities. In a recent interview, Richard Whiteley, author of *The Corporate Shaman*, theorized that this is a shamanic dismemberment—the experience of being taken apart, devoured, or torn to pieces on a global scale, allowing for a shift of awareness and transformation of collective consciousness.[2]

In a shamanic dismemberment, the individual dies the little death, which is the surrender of the ego. At its deepest level, the dismemberment experience dismantles our old identity. It is a powerful death-and-rebirth process. The experience of being stripped, layer by layer, down to bare bones forces us to examine the bare essence of what we truly are.

Anthropologist Felicitas Goodman, the modern discoverer of ritual trance and sacred postures, notes that Siberian shamans considered dismemberment to be an essential phase of initiation for healers. Goodman researched and explored ritual body postures as a means to achieve a bodily induced trance experience and discovered that this archetype appears to be universal. In her trance work with Westerners, those who experienced spontaneous dismemberment visions were invariably destined to become various kinds of healers.[3]

Completing this restorative rite is precisely the task of the shaman. As Joan Halifax explains in her book *Shamanic Voices*, "The shaman is a healed healer who has retrieved the broken pieces of his or her body and psyche and, through a personal rite of transformation, has integrated many planes of life experience: the body and the spirit, the ordinary and nonordinary, the individual and the community, nature and supernature, the mythic and the historical, the past, the present and the future."[4] The cure for dismemberment is remembering who we actually are. As Halifax puts it, "To bring back to an original state that which was in primordial times whole and is now broken and dismembered is not only an act of unification, but also a divine remembrance of a time when a complete reality existed."[5]

In his book, *2012: The Return of Quetzalcoatl*, Daniel Pinchbeck developed the hypothesis that we are undergoing a transition to a new realization of consciousness, which will be embodied by a new fundamental paradigm that takes into account what Carl Jung called "the reality of the psyche," which is to recognize that its contents have a living reality, along with new social, political, and economic systems that mesh with this realization. Pinchbeck sees the rapid evolution of technology as an expression of this unfolding of consciousness. The acceleration of planetary crises can either incite a planetary awakening and a shift into a regenerative planetary culture based on sustainable principles, or a destruction of human civilization in its current form, and perhaps extinction for our species.[6]

The emerging viewpoint coming from the shamanic community suggests the times we live in have an underworld theme of planetary and cosmological initiation. Entrance into the Lower World is most often precipitated by physical, psychological, emotional, or spiritual events that force the surrender of our ego. Who we believe ourselves to be is not who we really are. No matter how many years one has been expanding and developing their consciousness, no one is exempt from this shamanic death-and-rebirth. This is a shamanic initiation on the grandest cosmological scale.

The caveat is to not swing into polar extremes of grandiosity or deficiency. Many may view this as either an opportunity for transformation or detached withdrawal. Others may react from fear and view this as impending doom and gloom. Rather, view the melodramatic experience as a test of spiritual maturity. This provides the opportunity for letting go and surrendering our ego defensiveness.

The times we find ourselves in are like a great river in flood. We can try to hold on to trees or rocks on the shore to save ourselves from being swept along with the current. But this is a futile endeavor, for nothing can resist the great tide of change that is sweeping through and forever altering life as we have known it for tens of thousands of years on this planet.

Instead, we are being challenged to let go of the bank and let ourselves be swept along with the river, floating with the current, keeping our heads above the water, and trusting where the current might take us. We are being given the opportunity to surrender to the great tide of change, so that new dreams and visions can emerge. We can participate in the world's re-birth by following our own deepest instincts, each contributing our sacred part by following that which holds for us the greatest sense of truth and meaning.

The positive side of global dismemberment is that it eventually leads to a rebirth: to new ways of being. The darkness, which had seemed endless and impenetrable, is at long last revealed to be simply a very difficult passage—the proverbial tunnel, at the end of which is a brilliant, welcoming light.

SHAMANIC DRUMMING

Chapter 3

The Training

The shaman basically is an exemplar, a model, for how to be. The cultures that possess shamanism function—the entire culture—as a shamanic model for those of us who wander in the Prodigal's desert of materialism.
—Terrence McKenna[1]

Life goes on. Upon returning from my California trek, I found another retail job and pursued further research and studies. Though I did not fully comprehend the effects my spiritual calling had on me, my life began to change. Finding a meaningful path with purpose became my new quest. Collective archetypes began to reveal themselves to me in literature. I discovered renowned writer and mythologist Joseph Campbell and his vast work in comparative mythology and religion. Campbell mapped the cohesive threads in mythology that appeared to exist among even disparate human cultures. One of his pearls of wisdom resonated with me and became my new mantra: "Follow your bliss and the universe will open doors where there were only walls."

To follow your bliss, you must search within to find your innate gifts or passions, and then apply them in your life's work and your relationships. What is your deepest inner longing? What is it you wish to do more than anything else? Whatever it is, it will carry you to what you need to do next in order to fulfill your life's purpose, even if you don't yet know what that purpose is. When something is easily presented to you and it sounds like a wonderful and enjoyable thing to do, then by all means do it. That is guidance. What else is there to do in life but to follow one's joy and passion?

I found my true bliss exploring the natural world around me. I hiked, climbed, and backpacked at every opportunity. I eventually followed my bliss into the high desert of Central Oregon. After our first visit to this arid volcanic region, Elisia and I purchased some acreage near Newberry

Crater south of Bend, Oregon. It was here that I decided to build a cabin and settle down, or so I thought.

I spent the entire summer of 1981 camping in a tent on our wooded lot in Central Oregon. I declared my personal independence, immersed myself in nature, and constructed my own humble dwelling from the ground up. Like Henry David Thoreau, "I went to the woods because I wished to live deliberately, to front only the essential facts of life, and see if I could not learn what it had to teach, and not, when I came to die, discover that I had not lived."[2]

After settling into our forest cabin, I felt the urge to write again. Other than journaling and taking research notes, I had done very little writing since my college composition courses. As a freelance writer, I sold the first article I ever wrote. The title was "20/20 Vision Without Glasses." It appeared in the July/August 1983 Issue 82 of *The Mother Earth News*. I was ecstatic when the complimentary copies arrived in the mail. I was a published writer. More tailor written articles were published in other periodicals, but I was feeling a deeper calling.

Being of Native American descent, I was drawn to indigenous mythology, spirituality, and shamanism. I read the seminal books *Black Elk Speaks* by John G. Neihardt and *The Sacred Pipe* by Joseph Epes Brown. In my research, I discovered the work of influential Native American writers Vine Deloria, Jr., Leslie Marmon Silko, and N. Scott Momaday. I enjoyed reading the controversial other-worldly Carlos Castaneda books. I later read *Rolling Thunder* by Doug Boyd and Dhyani Ywahoo's insightful book *Voices of our Ancestors: Cherokee Wisdom Teachings from the Wisdom Fire*. What I learned from my studies is that indigenous people view the earth as a sentient being, seeing everything as interconnected, interdependent, and mutually supportive in the web of life. Ecology and shamanism shared similar holistic cosmologies.

A path with heart

In mid-March 1988, I met gemologist and psychic adept Doug Ward at his gem shop in Sunriver, Oregon. As I expressed in the Acknowledgments, "Doug Ward illuminated the path and showed me the way." At the time, I was writing an apocalyptic supernatural thriller. In the novel, I tried to integrate all of the things I had learned about the circle of life and its fragility. The heroes of my novel were shamans who intervened on behalf of Gaia to save humanity from its own undoing. They shamanized the Earth Mother at her holy places to harmonize the circle of life for optimal experience.

Doug told me that I would probably abandon the novel and write non-fiction books on shamanism. He also told me that I would most likely move to the American Southwest to study with a shaman, who was both a teacher and a student to me in past lives. Doug said that it could take years to meet this shaman. It all depended on my willingness to commit and make the necessary sacrifices.

Doug taught me the medicine of working with Stone People. Stone People contain the knowledge of Mother Earth and her evolution. Each type of stone person has its own energy, healing properties, and wisdom to share. They each bring unique lessons, whether they are a precious stone, gemstone, or just a piece of tumbled river rock. To learn from these ancient teachers, I had to learn to still my mind and listen closely. Doug taught me various methods of meditation, visualization, and how to sense and work with the subtle energies of stones.

This was a period of rapid inner growth for me. I was changing from the inside out. A shift in consciousness heightened my awareness and redefined my core values.

I was also tested. We are always tested by the spirits from time to time to see if we have a clear and open heart. You must show the spirit world that you have passion and heart. You must be willing to take risks. It never really ends. You must prove yourself again and again. A meaningful path must have heart. You must surrender the ego. You must give up the need for control.

I soon learned that walking a path with heart is not always peaceful and euphoric. As I learned to still my mind, my ego resisted, often creating illusory fears and nightmares in which I battled inner demons. The instinctual warning system meant to keep us safe from unknown dangers that lie beyond our senses can entrap us. In order to remain master, the ego can generate fears and even create bodily pain.

There was also growing tension in my marriage. I began to ask myself the same questions that the spirits were asking of me:

"Was I willing to commit to this shamanic path and make the necessary sacrifices?"

"Was I willing to take risks to meet my shamanic teacher?"

"Was I willing to move from my Northwest sanctuary to the Desert Southwest?"

"Was I willing to sell my cabin in the woods that I had built from the ground up?"

I was willing to do all of these to move forward. For me, it was an easy decision. For my wife, it was more agonizing. She was my reluctant partner on this spiritual quest, yet she too was being called by the spirits. She also was being tested. We were both being asked to sacrifice everything to be something we were not before.

Shamanic journeying

In May of 1988, a friend of Doug's introduced me to group journeying using the Michael Harner method. Founder of The Foundation for Shamanic Studies, Michael Harner is widely acknowledged as the world's foremost authority on shamanism and has had an enormous influence on both the academic and lay worlds. Harner teaches core shamanism, the universal, near-universal, and common methods of the shaman to enter non-ordinary reality for problem solving and healing. Particular emphasis is on the classic shamanic journey: one of the most remarkable visionary methods used by humankind to access inner wisdom and guidance by the teachers within. Learning to journey is the first step in becoming a shamanic practitioner. The exercises outlined in the next chapter will help you learn the basics of shamanic journeying.

Shamanism is based on the principle that the spiritual world may be contacted through the inner senses in ecstatic trance. Basically, shamanic journeying is a way of communicating with your inner or spirit self and retrieving information. Your inner self is in constant communication with all aspects of your environment, seen and unseen. You need only journey within to find answers to your questions. You should always journey with a purpose, question, or intention. After the journey, you must then interpret the meaning of your trance experience.

Drumming is a simple and effective way to induce this ecstatic trance state. When a drum is played at an even tempo of three to four beats per second for at least fifteen minutes, most novices report that they can journey successfully even on their first attempt. Transported by the driving beat of the shaman's drum; the shamanic traveler journeys into the spirit world and back.

The journey technique taught by Michael Harner is to visualize an opening into the earth that you remember from sometime in your life. The entrance could be an animal burrow or a cave. When the drumming begins, you go down the hole and a tunnel will appear. The tunnel often appears ribbed and may bend or spiral around. This tunnel-like imagery is related to the central axis that links the three inner planes of consciousness. Enter the tunnel and you will be conveyed up or down to an exit that opens out into mystical worlds.

In these worlds, the shaman experiences sensations and communications that go beyond the usual senses. Conversing with plants, animals, and the guiding forces of nature becomes possible. The shaman accesses knowledge, power, and healing. Upon finishing the explorations, he or she returns via the tunnel to ordinary reality. It is interesting to note that such tunnel imagery is prevalent among descriptions given of the near-death experience.

After a brief introduction to the Michael Harner method of journeying, the five of us sat in a circle listening to a shamanic drumming recording for around fifteen minutes. This was my first group journey experience and at the time seemed unproductive. I remember finding a coyote burrow and entering the earth, but I could not see anything beyond that or find my way into the tunnel leading to the spirit world. The trickster coyote opened a portal to other realms, but then kept me in the dark. The joke was on me.

Like developing any skill, journeying takes practice. It was not until I purchased a shamanic drumming recording that my ability to journey began to blossom. Shamanic drumming is drumming for the purpose of shamanic journeying. A good journey drumming recording should be pulsed at around three to four beats per second. At this cadence, a drum creates wonderful harmonics. Harmonics are the common characteristic in many sounds used for journeying: throat-singing, berimbau, singing bowls, and didgeridoo. You can experiment with different harmonic sounds and instruments to journey to. Out in nature, I have journeyed at different times listening to the sounds of cicadas, crickets, croaking frogs, waterfalls, and so on. Although other sounds can be used for journeying, drumming seems to be the one most often used throughout the world.

The way of the shaman

In June of 1988, I acquired and read *The Way of the Shaman* by Michael Harner. This informative guide to core shamanic practice set me on a new course in life. From this guide, I learned to hone my skills of shamanic journeying. I have always had a vivid imagination, so journeying comes easily for me. I close my eyes as if to sleep, and my inner world awakens.

Journey work is so therapeutic. It reconnects you with your inner or spirit self. The moment you bond with your spirit is the moment your heart opens. The first time you glimpse your spirit self, you gasp and cry. You know who you are. That is the moment you begin to heal.

For six months, I journeyed virtually every day. My trance experiences were healing and empowering. They often triggered the release of suppressed emotions, producing feelings of peace and well-being. The process restores emotional health through expression and integration of emotions.

Once I learned to journey, my shamanic training began. I sought out and met my spirit helpers and guardian spirit, the bear. I communed with the archetypal realms of the collective soul. The spirit world became my classroom and the spirits became my teachers.

My first powerful journeys took place outside in the wild. They were flights of the soul that I shall never forget. I remember riding my bicycle through the forest one summer day when an orange butterfly flew directly into my path.

The butterfly is an archetypal symbol of transformation, transmutation, and magic in world mythology and religion. When I encounter one of these remarkable beings, I stop and observe them carefully. I have learned to trust these endearing spirit guides. Butterflies have brought me messages from my ancestors and guided me to specific places of power in the web of life on many occasions.

The butterfly fluttered across the road and into the pine forest. I felt the urge to follow it. One of the things I have learned working with spirits is that they often prompt me, through urges, to do one thing or another. This is a common form of communication and instruction by helping spirits.

I got off my bike and pursued the butterfly into the woods on foot. When it paused or changed directions, so did I. If I lost sight of it, it would eventually reappear. Eventually, the butterfly led me to an area of disturbed soil under the forest canopy. I found several badger burrows dug into the sandy pumice soil. The energy felt different here. There was an electrical tingle in my hands and scalp. I knew instantly that this was a power place for me—a place to journey.

I returned the next day on my bike, bringing a Walkman cassette player and headphones so I could journey listening to the sound of drumming. I also brought a voice activated micro-cassette recorder so that I could narrate and record my journey as it transpired. This can be distracting at first, but it is one of the best ways I know to make sure you are getting all the information your helping spirits are giving you. On my first journey sitting near the entrance to a badger burrow, I encountered some very influential teachers:

Meeting my spirit guide

The drumbeats carried me away on the wings of an eagle. I soared high over South Sister (a volcanic peak in the Oregon Cascades) and then dove into a cave on her south flank. Clear quartz crystals shimmered from the walls, floor, and ceiling. I transformed into a man and followed a narrow path through the crystal cave. The path led me through a labyrinth of twists and turns until the cave ended abruptly in a wall of crystals. A small portal appeared in the wall and sucked my awareness into a dark tunnel. I spiraled downward and came out of the tunnel onto the rim of a red mesa. I saw a pueblo below me at the base of the mesa. I heard drumming and chanting and saw many dancers.

Suddenly, I became one of the dancers. I gazed at the man who played the booming drum. He wore a red headband. He smiled at me and chanted loudly. At the sound of his voice, I transformed into a golden eagle and took flight. I circled the pueblo and then glided over the desert. I soared towards the sun high above the earth. I saw the earth below transform into a beautiful clear quartz crystal.

I then folded my wings and plunged to the earth below. I flew across the desert to the ruins of an ancient cliff dwelling built high in the alcove of a limestone cliff. I flew into a doorway and transformed once again into a man. I looked at the floor of the room and saw the white bones of a human skeleton. The skeleton arose, transforming into a beautiful Pueblo women. She walked toward me and gently caressed my cheek with her hand. She smiled and said, "I am your guide."

I clasped her outstretched hand and we both transformed into golden eagles. We flew away from the cliff dwelling and soared high above the desert. As the sun began to set on the horizon, we separated and I returned rapidly to the red mesa above the pueblo. I entered a small portal in the top of the mesa and retraced the passage back to my body.

The spirit guide I encountered in the preceding journey became my mentor in the ways of the spirit world. Known as Corn Woman, or Corn Mother, she is an important deity archetype in Pueblo mythology. She represents fertility, life, and the feminine aspects of this world. The importance of corn deities in Pueblo mythology reflects the importance of corn in the Pueblo diet. Each pueblo performs a ritual Corn Dance to honor Corn Woman and pray for rain, growth, and fertility. A drummer and a chorus of chanting men support the lines of dancers who move in a continually changing zigzag pattern. The dancers make gestures to indicate their requests to Corn Woman: lowering the arms depicts the lowering clouds, moving the arms in a zigzag motion denotes lightning, lowering the palms signifies rain, and lifting the hands symbolizes the growing stalks of corn.[3]

The drummer I met in my spirit journey later manifested as a human guide in the physical world. Like the drummer in my journey, he wore a red bandana and carried a drum. The shaman's name is Jade Wah'oo Grigori and he mentored me in shamanic drumming.

Meeting my shamanic teacher

In November of 1988, Elisia and I sold our home and moved to Sedona, Arizona. I was on a spiritual quest and my wife was a reluctant companion. At that time, Sedona was becoming known as a "New Age Mecca," attracting pilgrims from around the world. I was one of those pilgrims. My artistic wife found work in one of Sedona's well known art galleries, and I found work as a bartender at a Sedona racquet club. Art and tennis funded our spiritual quests.

After several relatively uneventful months in Sedona, I finally had a profound shamanic experience. I attended my first shamanic drumming circle a few blocks from our apartment. I had picked up an event flyer in a neighborhood New Age bookstore which read:

Shamanic Drumming Circle. Jade Wah'oo Grigori is a traditional shaman of Mongolian ancestry. In keeping with his intent to make accessible to all peoples, regardless of blood line, the knowledge and practice of 'The Ways' of Shamanism, is calling forth a drum circle. Those of the community seeking to join together with others of like heart-beat in learning and experiencing the empowerment and filling of the light-body through shamanic drum ways, are invited to participate. Tuesday Nights, 7 p.m. to 9 p.m.

When I arrived at the host's house, I joined about fifteen people sitting casually in a semi-circle around the perimeter of the living room floor. Some people had drums and others did not. Most of the furniture had been removed to accommodate a large gathering. Two of the participants were percussionists who had just arrived in Sedona to give a performance at a local venue after the drum circle. They brought a wide assortment of frame and ethnic drums. They passed instruments around the circle so that everyone in our circle had a drum if they chose to play. I received a frame drum and beater as it came round the circle to me. I had never played a frame drum before. It was a very eclectic mix of people and rhythm instruments. I came to know a few of these participants very well in the months to come.

After our host introduced Jade, he entered the room and sat down. He was wearing a red bandana and carried a double-sided frame drum and a bound bundle. Jade laid out his drum and opened the bundle, laying power objects on a woven rug. He then lit a charcoal incense burner. In the darkened room, I could see blue sparks dance off of the charcoal as the sacred fire came to life. Jade then sprinkled herbs on the burning charcoal and began smudging his sacred objects with three feathers, fanning the smoke outward into the entire space. Smudging is the burning of herbs or incense for cleansing, purification, and protection of sacred space. After smudging, Jade recounted the mythic telling of shamanic creation, when human beings were one of the Animal Brothers:

Grandfather fire and the circle of animal brothers

In that time before there was Time, there was Grandfather Fire. Around Grandfather Fire sat the Circle of Animal Brothers, and beyond them ... the Darkness.

In the Circle of Animal Brothers, there was Eagle, Raven, Owl, and then there was Gander. There was Bear, Panther, Deer, and then there was Horse. There was Turtle, Fire Lizard, Snake, and then there was Spider. There was the Two-Legged. And each in their turn spoke their Tellings in the common yet sacred language of Spirit. Through these Tellings, Grandfather Fire gave rise to the nature of Creation.

There came Time when the Two-Leggeds got up and left the Circle. Nobody knows why they left the Circle. Maybe they had to take a leak behind a bush. No one knows. After some time had passed, their absence was noted. Then the members of the Circle of Animal Brothers began to wonder amongst themselves and expressed their wonderment, in addition to their original Tellings.

"I wonder where our Brothers have gone?"

"I wonder where those Two-Leggeds are? I saw them get up and leave the Circle."

"I wonder ... what is it that is beyond the Circle."

"The Darkness"

"I wonder why it is dark? What is this thing, Darkness? Why does it lie beyond our Circle? Why have our Brothers, the Two-Leggeds, wandered into this place of darkness? Why have they gone and left our Circle open?"

Grandfather Fire, hearing these additions to the original Tellings, and noticing the resultant alterations in the unfolding of Creation, then called upon his best hunter and seeker of the night to go in search of the Two-Leggeds. For that purpose, he chose Owl.

Owl, who can sense everything in the darkness, searched and searched throughout his entire hunting domain. Owl, not finding his Brothers, called out, "Grandfather, my Brothers, I can find the Two-Leggeds nowhere. They must be dead!"

And so it was, and so it is, and so shall it ever be that Owl is the harbinger of Death.

Now the members of the Circle of Animal Brothers, in addition to their original Tellings in that original and sacred language of Spirit, began to question amongst themselves, "What is this thing, Death?"

"Where in the Darkness is Death?"

"Why is Death in association with the Darkness?"

"What of our Brothers, the Two-Leggeds? Why have they left the Circle? Why have they gone into the Darkness? Why have they gone to this place of Death? What is it about this thing Death that so holds their attention? What is it about Death that can so hold our Brothers that they would leave our Circle wounded?"

Grandfather Fire, hearing these even further additions and alterations to the original and sacred Tellings, chose his most beautiful of all creations to go in search of the Two-Leggeds. He chose the one whose every single feather was glistening, gleaming silver. He chose Raven.

He sent Raven forth through the darkness. Raven flew for Time upon Time, aeon upon aeon, until at last, coming through the slamming rocks at the Gates of Death, Raven slipped through and into the Land of Death, that the Two-Leggeds had come to refer to as Life.

Searching, Raven finds his Brothers the Two-Leggeds, and finding them, calls out, "My brothers! My brothers! I found you! I found you at last! Come home, come home, come home!"

The Two-Leggeds, they look up and see Raven flying overhead and they hear him calling out, "Caaaaaaaaaaw–ahaaaaaaaa! Caaaaaw! Caaaaaaaaaaaaw–aaww-awww–aaww-awww!"

Raven understands then that the Two-Leggeds had lost their ability to communicate in the common yet sacred language of Spirit.

Raven, so that his Brothers in the Circle might know for themselves the state and condition of the Two-Leggeds, places in his beak some of that stickiness that is uniquely human: Sadness and Despair (which is to say: Emotion). With that, Raven slips back through the slamming rocks at the Gates of Death and sets forth upon his return journey to Grandfather Fire and the Circle of Animal Brothers.

As Raven flew, the stickiness drew upon his life force and as it drew, it grew and it grew, becoming heavier and heavier. Raven flew lower and lower. Deeper and deeper and deeper into the Darkness Raven flew. Soon the stickiness filled Raven. So greatly did it draw upon his life force, so great did it grow, that it began to exude from within him until his every single bright, glistening, gleaming silvery feather was covered with stickiness, and to that stickiness clung the Darkness. By the time that Raven had returned to the

Circle of Animal Brothers and Grandfather Fire, he was dark as the Night itself.

Upon his return, so that each might know for themselves the condition of their Brothers the Two-Leggeds, Raven took from his beak that stickiness, and passed it around. Each of the members of the Circle of Animal Brothers in their turn felt of it, smelled of it, and tasted it; then passed it around the Circle.

And now, each of the Animal Brothers, having imbibed of the stickiness of emotion, in addition to their Tellings in the common and sacred language of Spirit, began to discuss among themselves what must be done.

"You know, we're going to have to go and bring our Brothers back."

"No, no, this we cannot do. For we ourselves would have to leave our Circle."

"Then leave our Circle we must. We've got to get them back."

"No, no, you don't understand. If we were to leave the Circle, then we must ourselves go into the Darkness."

"Then into the Darkness we must go."

"No, no, no. What if we go into the Darkness? Then, into the Land of Death we would have to go to find our Brothers."

"Then into the Land of Death we must go."

"No, no, no. For then we ourselves would die."

"Then that is a risk we must take; we must risk Death itself to bring our Brothers back home."

"No, no, no, this we cannot do."

"But we must do this. We have a responsibility to them."

"We have no responsibility to them. They are the ones who left our Circle of their own accord. Let them find their own way back."

"No, no, no Brothers, we have to bring them back."

"No they are the ones who left and broke our Circle."

Grandfather Fire, hearing them argue in this manner, knew then that something must be done.

And so, he called forth his grandest of all creations. He called forth the Eagle. Grandfather Fire passed his presence into the Eagle.

Eagle flew through the Darkness along the pathway that Raven had described, and in an instant-less-than-an-instant Eagle flew through the Darkness, through the slamming rocks at the Gates of

Death, and into the Land of Death itself, the place that the Two-Leggeds had come to call Life.

Eagle landed. As his talons touched the Earth, he took on the form of a human, the one we refer to as Eagle Brother/First Shaman. This he did to bring to the people, 'the Ways.' This he did so that through the application of 'the Ways,' each would have the opportunity of seeking and finding fulfillment of their own unique path of reunification with Grandfather Fire. That is, that we, who are here on the Earth—our Grandmother, the primordial feminine principle of Creator—would have available to us the methods and techniques, songs, ceremonies and meditations through whose application we would each be enabled in our Quest for our own Spirit's Truth, our own autonomous path of Self-Realization; our path of return to Grandfather Fire—the primordial masculine principle of Creator. The gift of Eagle was given so that we, who are here in the flesh, would awaken as Spirit.

Furthermore, Eagle Brother/First Shaman chose twelve humans from amongst those on the planet and initiated them, passing into their caretakership 'the Ways,' giving them instruction in the initiation of their successors, in the transmission of these Ways down through the twelve lineages established, so that all across the Earth, throughout the many, many, many generations to come, 'the Ways' would be accessible; so that any person of sincerity, commitment, integrity, dedication, from anywhere upon this planet, at any time, who would seek to avail themselves of these ways, would find that opportunity. These are the ways of Eagle Brother, First Shaman.[4]

Gift of the drum

Upon finishing the mythic telling of "Grandfather Fire and the Circle of Animal Brothers," Jade held up his drum and continued:

There came a time when Eagle Brother brought to us the Shamanic Drum. It is the Shaman's foremost vehicle for engaging one's attention in spiritual upliftment, for the gift of the drum is that it enables us to once again communicate in the Sacred Language of Spirit! A thorough understanding of the phenomena associated with the experience of Shamanic Drumming must include an integration of both the physiological and the transcendent.

SHAMANIC DRUMMING

A Shamanic Drum is constructed within very precise parameters for maximum effectiveness. The rim is made of wood, usually cedar, or a local wood with good resonate qualities. The coverings are most typically of elk or deer rawhide. A rim three to four inches in height by 17 or 18 inches in diameter provides the proper dimensional relationships for the qualities desired in a Shamanic Drum. When a drum of these materials and dimensions is played, it offers qualities of tone unlike any other drum, even the one-sided hand drum that many people nowadays are using.

When a Shamanic Drum is struck upon one side, it produces the sound of the beat, and a primary tone, or resonance. Since the hides covering the two sides of the drum are never able to be strung to precisely the same tautness, one side will always have a slightly higher pitch than the other side. The primary tone on the higher-pitched side will, consequently, have a "ring" to it. When the lower-pitched side is struck, a lower "drone" is produced in addition to the beat. Because of the close proximity of the hides to each other, being only three to four inches apart, when one side of the drum is struck, the sound wave of that strike impacts the other side's hide, causing it to resonate as well. We now have three tones being produced simultaneously from one strike: the beat, the primary tone (either a "ring" or a "drone," depending on which side is struck) and the secondary resonance of the opposing hide's vibration.

The human mind fixates upon the monotonous and repetitive. The constant striking of the drum produces a repetitive and monotonous beat pattern. When the mind fixates, all "chitter-chatter" and emotional overwhelm ceases. A profound state of Silence ensues.

The high-pitched overtone stimulates the brain into the alpha brain wave state. This alpha state is experienced as a dreamy, daydream-like state of being. Physiologically, our response to the alpha state is a deep physical relaxation, which comes over us. A daydream's content is driven by the emotionally laden internal dialogue going on within us. Because the mind is fixated, there is nothing to drive any content. In this way, Shamanic Drumming produces a daydream state of alpha without emotional content.

The undertone "drone" produced in Shamanic Drumming stimulates the brain into the theta brain wave state. Though this is characterized as the deep dreaming state, the most relevant response is that the drone opens our spiritual heart, allowing our indwelling presence of being, our Spirit, to rise forth unimpeded.

When these three states of consciousness—silence, alpha and theta—occur simultaneously, as in Shamanic Drumming, a phenomenal experience proceeds. The Spirit, rising forth through the now opened heart, is freed to express itself. The Spirit expresses itself through image, symbols, song/chant, tones, colors, sensations and knowingness. Where does the Spirit express itself? In the now empty alpha daydream state. The mind, fixated and silent, cannot help but pay attention to that which is transpiring within the alpha state. We are now able to perceive directly the expressions, or desires, of our Spirit—that is, we are now able to once again communicate in the Sacred Language of Spirit!

What had become lost to us, due to the spiritual amnesia inherent within incarnation in the mundane world, is now directly accessible to us once again—through the direct experience of Shamanic Drumming![5]

Double-headed drums

Jade explained that a double-headed drum is preferred by some shamans, for it constitutes a microcosm of the universe, unites the masculine and feminine principles, and produces sounds with a tremendous dynamic range. The higher-pitched head of the drum tends to affect higher levels of consciousness. Typically, shamans associate this drumhead with the sky, Upper World, and masculine energy. It is linked to the mythic Spirit Eagle that perches atop the World Tree. Eagle Brother will carry the shaman's prayers to the Upper World, or the shaman may transform into Spirit Eagle and soar into the Celestial Realm. The shaman and Eagle are both intercessors between the Celestial and human realms.

The opposite or lower-pitched head of the drum affects deeper levels of consciousness. It is commonly associated with the Lower World, feminine energy, and the archetypal Horse of mythology. The repetitive, droning rhythm of shamanic drumming is suggestive of a horse on a journey. Throughout Mongolia, shamans describe it as the exalted, buoyant state that one mounts and rides from plane to plane. Mongolian shamans ride Spirit Horse, called *Omisi Murin*, into the Lower World on healing journeys or direct Spirit Horse to carry the power and healing to the intended destination.

The rim of the drum symbolizes the Middle World and is connected to the World Tree through the wood of the frame and its association through all trees back to the First Tree. Like the World Tree, which links the Earth and Sky, the rim links the two sides of the drum—the yin and the yang. A double-headed drum unites the feminine and masculine aspects of the universe within itself. It restores the balance of these polar, yet co-creative elements.

Unlike a single-headed drum, which has no space in its design to store energy, a double-headed drum is able to hold power, which is utilized in certain shamanic work. When playing a two-headed drum, you can feel the energy you generate move from the head being struck to the opposite head, resonate it, then bounce back and out. As percussionist Sule Greg Wilson puts it, "You should feel an echo, a rebound of sound within the drum's shell. That way the energy circulates, comes back, and you can use it again."[6] You know that you are playing the drum correctly when you feel that subtle kickback in your hands or on the drumstick and hear the drum shell ringing. The whole drum needs to sing.

The key is to focus your energy to that point on the drumhead's surface that you are striking, not beyond it. Transfer your energy and intention into the drum, stroking it firmly, yet gently, until it sings and hums. This technique applies to playing any drum. With practice, you learn just how much energy to send out to achieve a desired result and how much to retain so that you don't tire.

Three-sided shamanic drum journey

Jade instructed us in the ritual use of the sacrament tobacco, the unifying thread of communication between humans and the spiritual powers. He showed us how to empower our drums by offering tobacco smoke or a pinch of dry tobacco. Offering grandfather tobacco carries our prayers to the "Loom of Creation," causing the "Tapestry of Creation" to reweave itself in accordance with those prayers.

Next, Jade taught us the drum beats for invoking Eagle Brother and Spirit Horse. After learning the two rhythms, Jade led us in a three round shamanic drum journey. During the first round, we drummed the eagle-beat on the Celestial (higher-pitched) head of our drums and journeyed into the Upper World. In the second round, we drummed the horse-beat on the Lower World (lower-pitched) head of our drums and rode Spirit Horse on a journey into the Lower World. In the third round, we switched back to the Celestial side of our drums and again drummed the eagle-beat, offering prayers of thanks and gratitude to Eagle Brother and Spirit Horse for their help and assistance. Finally, Jade signaled the end of our journey and the drum circle with four strong beats.

I was transformed by the power of that drum circle—it was a defining moment in my life. The vibrant energy was unifying, expansive, and palpable. I could feel the spirits in the room. Shamanic drumming shook the earth beneath me, split me wide open, and lifted my spirit skyward. The ecstatic rhythms resonated to my very core. From that point on, I was hooked on sonics!

The next day, I went back to the store where I had picked up the drum circle flyer and purchased an octagonal double-sided frame drum. I returned week after week to Jade's shamanic drumming circles to learn and experience more drum ways. Under Jade's tutelage, I learned the myths, healing rhythms and drum ways of an ancient shamanic lineage. Through drumming, I found a meaningful way to express myself without words. More importantly, I discovered my true calling—shamanic drumming.

Finding my own path

After six months in Sedona, Elisia and I both felt the inner urge to travel again. I found myself in a dilemma, torn between embarking on another travel adventure and pursuing a shamanic apprenticeship; each appealed to me. I asked myself, "Do I want to be a nomad or a shaman, or are they the same thing?" I decided to consult the I Ching to gain some insight into my situation.

The I Ching is an ancient Chinese text and divination system which counsels appropriate action in the moment for a given set of circumstances. Each moment has a pattern to it and everything that happens in that moment is interconnected. Based on the synchronicity of the universe and the laws of probability, the I Ching responds to an inquiry in the form of a hexagram. By evaluating the hexagram that describes your current pattern of relationship, you can divine the outcome and act accordingly.

The I Ching is a microcosm of all possible human situations. It serves as a dynamic map, whose function is to reveal one's relative position in the cosmos of events. When I consulted the I Ching regarding my situation, I received hexagram 61 Inner Truth. The hexagram's judgment was:

Good fortune.
It furthers one to cross the great water.
Perseverance furthers.

This hexagram had one changing line in the third place which read:

He finds a comrade.
Now he beats the drum, now he stops.
Now he sobs, now he sings.

Changing lines usually address the future implications of a particular course of action. They may describe the changes you are likely to experience and how to deal with them. The commentary describing this changing line read:

Here the source of a man's strength lies not in himself but in his relation to other people. No matter how close to them he may be, if his center of gravity depends on them, he is inevitably tossed to and fro between joy and sorrow. Rejoicing to high heaven, then sad unto death—this is the fate of those who depend upon an inner accord with other persons whom they love. Here we have only the statement of the law that this is so. Whether this condition is felt to be an affliction of the supreme happiness of love, is left to the subjective verdict of the person concerned.[7]

I was thunderstruck by the insight and clarity of this I Ching reading. The drumming metaphor could not have been more relevant to my situation. This line underscores the importance of maintaining our center of gravity or inner independence in our relationships with others. The power of inner truth depends upon it. Inner truth refers to what we inwardly know to be true. Those who depend upon an inner accord with others risk being tossed to and fro between joy and sorrow. The hexagram seemed to be saying, "You know what the problem is, and you understand the truth of the matter."

I interpreted this as meaning that, though I had found a comrade and teacher, it was time to part ways. I had a deep respect for the powerful rhythms and drum ways of Jade's tradition, but I had to follow my own path of rhythm. As philosopher Terrence McKenna put it, "Shamanism is a call to authenticity ... to discover something authentic."[8]

In June of 1989, Elisia and I had a yard sale, hauled the remainder of our belongings to a storage unit in Sedona, and set off on another adventure. We traveled the west, visiting national parks and camping for the summer. I drummed everywhere we traveled. Though Jade was my mentor, the drum became my teacher and creative addiction. I developed an insatiable thirst for its rhythms. I became a rhythm seeker, learning new rhythms from nature, dreams, and visions.

At the end of the summer, Elisia and I retrieved our belongings from storage in Sedona and returned to Bend, Oregon to make yet another fresh start. Upon our return, I found work as a seasonal Forest Service technician. I gradually processed my shamanic experiences and then tried to integrate what I had learned into a meaningful, authentic life. My deepest passion, then and now, is to express myself through shamanic drumming. Drumming became my vehicle for connecting with spirit and community. I began making rawhide frame drums from deer and elk hides. Birthing shamanic drums became a passion that continues to this day.

Inspired by my shamanic experiences, I began writing again. Jade's ancient knowledge of drumming and healing rhythms was most influential in putting together my first book on shamanic drumming. I founded Talking Drum Publications in 1991 with the release of *The Shamanic Drum: A Guide to Sacred Drumming.*[9] Soon after the book's publication, I began teaching shamanic drumming through hands-on experiential workshops.

As a shamanic teacher and writer, my responsibility is to provide tools and techniques designed to bring the aspirant into contact with their helping spirits, securing a solid foundation upon which to build a spiritual practice. Once you have learned the basic skills, your helping spirits can provide you all the training you need. It is now time to renew your connection with your spirit helpers, teachers, and guides.

Chapter 4

Helping Spirits

The spirits are teachers, not therapists. They are here to teach us to be better humans.
—Christina Pratt, shamanic teacher and author[1]

For six months in 2005, I worked as a medical transport driver, assisting clients to and from doctor appointments. The work was very rewarding and I met interesting people from all walks of life. I am truly amazed at how people cope with their illnesses and disabilities. The human spirit is simply irrepressible.

I had an incredible experience one day after dropping a client off at a local hospital. As I got back in the car and sat down in the driver's seat, I got the sensation that someone or something was in the car with me. I closed my eyes, stilled my mind, and tuned in to what was happening. To my surprise, I discovered a huge spirit bear sitting in the back seat directly behind me. He was a jovial character and not the least bit menacing. I knew at once that he was a spirit helper there to aid the sick.

Sitting next to the bear was the spirit of a recently deceased friend. Sandy was a long-standing community drum keeper and a compassionate healer when she walked the earth in the flesh. In her hospice work, she had assisted folks in their death journey to the other side. She often worked with bear medicine in her psychopomp work, and the bear spirit was her traveling companion.

Sandy had first appeared to me several weeks earlier at the home of my dear friend Judith Thomson in Packwood, Washington. I was performing a drum therapy treatment on Judith's neighbor. I was drumming the bear-beat and singing a bear chant. Spirit Bear filled me in a powerful way and Sandy came through me as well. She performed some potent healing work on the client. Before she left, Sandy told me that she would be available to help me whenever I needed assistance in my healing work.

I was overjoyed to see Sandy once again. I asked her what she was up to. She said that she was there to help the sick and the dying. She advised me to call upon her and my other helping spirits daily to ride around in the taxi with me. She assured me that they would provide whatever help and healing they could for my clients.

I then began each morning with a prayer to my helping spirits, asking them to assist me, not only with my clients, but with my driving skills as well. I was not always aware of who was in the car with me or what was transpiring in the spirit realm. I had to focus on my driving, and it is not a good idea to enter altered states while operating a motor vehicle. Occasionally, I would get a glimpse of a spirit coming or going.

On one memorable occasion, I was driving a dialysis patient from Salem to Portland, Oregon. She sat in the front seat beside me and soon nodded off into a deep sleep. It was not unusual for my clients to fall asleep while the spirits performed their healing work. Shortly after she fell asleep, an enormous serpent slithered over the front seat and coiled around her body. The serpent worked on her for the entire ride to Portland. The energy in the cab was palpable. I was witness to an incredible and powerful treatment. It was an uplifting and unforgettable experience.

At times, I sensed dark and ominous beings leaving the cab after they had been extricated from clients. At other times, I sensed an entire entourage of spirits riding around with me or accompanying me as I walked through various hospitals and clinics. I have seen spirit wolves, lions, eagles, hawks, and horses. I once saw a very protective black jaguar watching over an infant boy with respiratory problems.

I never imagined when I started driving medical transport that it would become such an inspirational and rewarding experience. I thanked the spirits each day for the opportunity to help others and for this wonderful gift of life. Riding with the spirits was a fulfilling journey into the heart of community

Spirit helpers

Whether you realize it or not, you have always had helping spirits. Helping spirits are like family and friends, and each has a unique personality. Basically, a spirit helper is a coherent energy pattern that may take form as an animal, plant, ancestor, deity, element, or even a mythical creature such as a unicorn or dragon.

Mythical creatures manifest in our conscious, mythic awareness because they still exist in the Lower World. The same holds true for creatures that lived in the past and that are now extinct. A group archetype or oversoul of each extinct species continues to exist in the Lower World, so a person may have a dinosaur or mammoth as a power animal.

All helping spirits are extensions of the "one spirit" that pervades all existence, whom we could call God, the Tao, or Great Mystery. Spirits are a natural manifestation of human consciousness. They manifest in two main categories: those who have physical form and those who do not or no longer do. Those helping spirits that have a physical form are known as elementals and may include representatives of the plant, animal, or mineral kingdoms, or an element such as air, water, fire, earth, sun, moon, planets, stars, and so on.

Spirit helpers that do not operate out of the physical realm may include ancestors who choose to be of service to us or divine archetypes such as angels and devas. In the cultures of the past, these typically were the gods and goddesses of the Upper World. These helping spirits can take on a human form temporarily and act as intermediaries between us and the powers of the universe. They may include great spiritual teachers such as Jesus, Buddha, Lao-Tzu, and so on.

Trees and plants also manifest as helping spirits. Plant spirits are one of the major allies of shamans for healing, seeing, dreaming, and empowerment. Shamans heal using their knowledge of plant spirits as well as the plant's medicinal properties. When the shaman does not know what plant medicine to use for a sick person, the spirit of the plant tells him. Plants, however, are more than their chemical components. They are intelligent beings that have the capacity to raise consciousness to a level where true healing can take place. Plants have always evolved before their animal counterparts and offer profound guidance regarding our own spiritual evolution.

The majority of helping spirits take animal forms called power animals. Power animals are also called guardian spirits, spirit allies, totem animals, and tutelary animals. A power animal is the archetypal oversoul that represents the entire species of that animal. It is actually the spirit of one of the First People, as they are called, who at the end of mythic times turned into the animals as we know them today.

The mythology and creation stories of all Earth peoples speak of a primordial, but now lost paradise—a Garden of Eden in which humanity lived in harmony with all that existed. The cosmos had total access to itself. There was but one language for all creatures and elements. Humans were able to converse with animals, birds, minerals, and all living things. As respected Nakoda elder John Snow puts it, "We talked to the rocks, the streams, the trees, the plants, the herbs, and all nature's creations. We called the animals our brothers. They understood our language; we understood theirs. Sometimes they talked to us in dreams and visions. At times they revealed important events or visited us on our vision quests to the mountain tops."[2]

Animal characters played a prominent role in mythology. They were often portrayed as essentially human in bodily makeup, but possessed the individual characteristics of animals as they exist in nature today. Thus, Coyote is distinguished in the tellings by its mischievous behavior and Eagle by its great vision and ability to fly high into the sky realm of the Creator. Then, according to various cultural myths, the animals evolved into the forms in which they are found today. Raven, for example, is embodied in each individual member of the raven species, but Raven himself still lives in mythic times.

In the worldview of the shaman, power animals or animal archetypes such as Eagle, Coyote, and Bear represent and protect their entire species. When you connect with a power animal, you align yourself with the collective strength and wisdom of the entire species. One of the most important gifts that animal allies offer is protection and guardianship to the shaman during arduous shamanic tasks. Without this alliance, it is widely accepted that it is impossible to become a shaman.

Power animals are themselves great teachers and shamans. In many shamanic cultures, the knowledge imparted by a power animal is considered more important than the practical guidance of a master shaman. Power animals are valuable allies who can help you navigate through life's challenges and transitions. Many animals will come to guide you, some briefly and others throughout your life.

Power animals offer humans a much needed medicine. They remind us of what is innocent and truthful. Animals subsist from the heart, with a deep instinctual knowing that is always connected to the web of life. They live from the heart and are not entrapped by their reason. Humans, on the other hand, tend to live from the head, trying to figure everything out. But the energy that comes in from the source is directed through our hearts. We come into our own power when we learn to live from the heart. The heart attunes us to the flow of a dynamic, interrelated universe, helping us feel connected rather than isolated and estranged.

Communicating with helping spirits

Imagination is the key to communicating with the unseen world. Our imagination shapes our lives. It is with this understanding that William Blake said, "The imagination is not a State: it is the human existence in itself." If a shaman wants to retrieve information or a lost guardian spirit, "imagining what to look for" is the first step in achieving any result. The imagination is a means of communication, which developed much earlier than language and uses different neural pathways for the transmission of information.

This preverbal imagery is both personal and transpersonal. On a personal level, the imagination affects one's physical health and well-being. Images communicate with muscles, organs, and cells to effect a change. To experience this for yourself, try the following exercise:

1. Sit comfortably erect in your chair and turn your head as far as you can to the left and look straight ahead. Find something in your line of sight that you can remember as a benchmark for how far your head turned, and then bring your head forward again.
2. Now close your eyes, keep your head still, and imagine that you are slowly turning your head to the left very easily and loosely, without any strain, way past the benchmark until you are looking directly behind you without any problem at all. Imagine the sensation and feeling as well as the sight. Then imagine bringing your head slowly back to the front.
3. Now open your eyes and physically turn your head as far as you can to the left. Your line of sight should now be well past the benchmark.

Imagery is transpersonal in that it enables us to perceive and connect with alternate dimensional realities. One of the most crucial aspects of shamanic practice is the development of inner vision. In trance states, shamans develop such vivid internal imagery that external sensory input and bodily sensations are blocked out. Once vivid life like imagery is experienced, the next phase of practice is to develop control over the internal imagery. By orchestrating the inner imagery, the shaman is able to communicate with spirit guides and power animals. Over a period of time, the shaman develops the ability to see past, present, and future events. In these trance states, the shaman accumulates knowledge and inner power and is capable of influencing events for social benefit.

Inner vision is the portal through which we can experience the spirit world. The key is to create multidimensional images in your mind using sound, smell, taste, and touch, as well as sight. For example, if you were to envision an apple, you would see it, hold and feel it, smell it, and hear the crunch as you took a bite and tasted it. The ability to create multidimensional images is vital to successful journeying. Like developing any skill, visioning takes practice. Exercising your imagination through visioning develops your ability to journey. The following exercise is designed to acquaint you with the basics of shamanic visioning. The steps are as follows:

1. First, select an object in your home.
2. Sit comfortably with the object in your line of sight.
3. Take several deep breaths and exhale any tension you might feel.
4. Gaze at the object for a few moments.
5. Close your eyes and visualize the object as clearly as possible, including every detail that you can remember. If you need to refresh your memory, open your eyes and look at the object again.
6. When you have created the most vivid image that you can, begin to focus on each part of it using all of the senses. Observe every quality: size, shape, color, texture, feel, sound, smell, taste.
7. Now vividly imagine with every sense making changes to the object. Change the feel, sound, scent, flavor, and appearance of the object. Spend as much time with this imagery as you would like.

Meeting your power animal

Now that you are familiar with the basics of creating multidimensional images, you can begin to manipulate the visionary content. By consciously interacting with the internal imagery, you will be able to meet and acquire your power animal or guardian spirit. The practice of shamanism is one of direct revelation and therefore anyone can find and meet their spirit animal. Most shamanic cultures believe that one is born with a guardian spirit—that at the moment of birth, one's power animal is born in the wild.

One may have several power animals over the course of a lifetime and never realize it. One has as many animal spirits as volunteer themselves.

We long ago lost our ability to communicate with the animal spirits. Recognizing and acquiring one's guardian spirit is an important aspect of shamanic practice. The most well known method of acquiring a power animal is the vision quest or vigil conducted in a remote wilderness location where one evokes the spirits through fasting and prayer. Another method is the shamanic journey.

Learning to journey is the first step in establishing a relationship with a power animal. To enter a trance state and support your journey, you will need a drum or a shamanic drumming recording. Shamanic drumming is drumming for the purpose of shamanic journeying. A good shamanic drumming recording should be pulsed at around three to four beats per second. You may also rattle, chant, or sing to induce trance. There is no right or wrong way to journey. Be innovative and try different ways of journeying. Many people need to move, dance, or sing their journeys. My first journeys were supported by listening to a shamanic drumming recording, but now I have stronger journeys when I drum for myself.

Another way to train yourself to focus and concentrate is to narrate your journey as you are experiencing it. To set this up, you need headphones to listen to the drumming recording and a recorder of some kind. The simultaneous narration and recording technique can be distracting at first, but it is one of the best ways I know to make sure you are getting all the information your helping spirits are giving you.

The spirit journey is not always what people expect, and sometimes there is uncertainty as to what one should experience in altered states. The ecstatic trance is an individual journey into non-ordinary reality; therefore, experiences vary from person to person and from journey to journey. Once you enter a trance state, the rhythm or sound of the drum tends to change. The drumbeat may appear to speed up or slow down, while the sound may grow louder, softer, or disappear. You may experience a change in body temperature, feel energy flowing through your body, or find yourself twitching, swaying, or rocking. It is not uncommon to hear sounds or voices. You may even smell specific aromas. You may see colorful patterns, symbolic images, or dreamlike visions. Some people may find that they have a highly developed inner vision, while others may rely more on an inner voice of insight, or an inner feeling of certainty. The key is to observe whatever happens without trying to analyze the experience.

During the spirit journey, one's awareness transcends ordinary reality. In journeys to the Lower World, one may experience the sensation of falling, sliding, or spiraling downward into or under the earth. In Upper World journeys, one may experience the sensation of rising, floating, flying, or spiraling upward through the air or sky.

I used a journey technique taught by Michael Harner the first time I journeyed. In his book, *The Way of the Shaman*, Harner recommends that you visualize an opening into the earth that you remember from sometime in your life—from childhood, or yesterday. Any entry into the ground will do—an animal burrow, hollow tree stump, cave and so on. When the drumming begins, you go down the hole and a tunnel will appear. The tunnel sometimes appears ribbed and may bend or spiral around. This tunnel-like imagery is associated with the central axis that unites the three inner planes of consciousness. Enter the tunnel and you will emerge into the journey landscape. The basic steps are as follows:

1. The first step is to select a private and quiet space. Make whatever arrangements are necessary to assure that you will not be disturbed. No phones, no interruptions.
2. Next, you should smudge the space, yourself, and your drum with the smoke of an herb. Smudging is a method of using smoke from burning herbs to purify a space in preparation for spiritual or inner work. The sacred smoke dispels any stagnant or unwanted energy and opens the energy channels of your body. Sage, cedar, and sweetgrass are traditionally used for smudging, but any dried herb is acceptable. Light the herbs in a fire-resistant receptacle and then blow out the flames. Then use a feather or your hands to draw the smoke over your heart, throat, and face to purify the body, mind, and spirit. Next, smudge your drum by passing it through the smoke. Conclude the smudging by thanking the plant or tree spirit whose body made the cleansing possible.
3. After smudging, dim the lights and sit comfortably in a chair or on the floor. Close your eyes and focus on the breath as it enters the nose and fills your lungs, then gently exhale any tension you might feel. Continue this breathing exercise until you are calm and relaxed.
4. Once you are fully relaxed, it is important to frame a simple and clear statement of your intent. You should always journey with a purpose, question, or intention. You might phrase your intention something like, "I choose to meet my power animal."

5. The next step is to enter a trance state. Either listen to a shamanic journey drumming recording, or begin drumming a steady, metronome-like pattern at a tempo of about three to four beats per second. This rapid eagle-beat creates the sensation of inner movement, which, if you allow it, will carry you along. Close your eyes, focus your attention on the sound of the drum, and vividly imagine with every sense the entrance to a cave or an opening in the earth that you have seen or visited. Clear your mind of everything but this image.

6. Approach the entrance or opening and enter it. Typically, someone or something will be waiting there to guide you. It may appear to you as an animal, a person, a light, a voice, or have no discernable form at all. If you are uncomfortable or put off by whatever appears, ask it to take another form. It is important that you see, feel, hear, or in some way sense the presence of a spirit guide that you trust and feel at ease with before proceeding with your journey. If you do not, then come back through the entrance and journey another time.

7. When you are ready to proceed, state your intention to the spirit guide and begin the journey. Follow your guide's lead and instructions in every respect. If asked to leave, do so at once. If the spirit waiting to guide you is an animal, ask it, "Are you my power animal?" It might answer you telepathically, or it might lead you somewhere and show you something. If it indicates that it is not your helping spirit, ask it to take you to your power animal. Your spirit guide may ask you to accompany it in some fashion. Typically, you will proceed rapidly down a passage or tunnel. If you encounter an obstacle, just go around it or look for an opening through it.

8. When you emerge from the tunnel, you will find yourself in the Lower World. It is here that you will find your power animal. Allow a landscape to materialize before you. It can be a desert, a forest, a beach, or a wilderness area that you have seen or visited. To make it more real, infuse your vision with all the sensations you can muster.

9. Then allow an image of an animal to appear in that landscape. Should a spirit animal present itself, ask it, "Are you my power animal?" Listen carefully to its response, and don't worry if you feel like you are just making up the answers. It often feels this way in the beginning. Be open to the sensations and feelings of being that animal. It is not uncommon to be and see the animal simultaneously. Moreover, it is best to avoid menacing animals with bared fangs. Such animals represent

obstacles and challenges to be confronted at a time when you have the assistance of a power animal.

10. Next, thank the animal for its assistance, and then allow the image of that animal to fade and another image to open up before you. Repeat this imagery with as many different animals as you wish. The key to recognizing your power animal is that it will repeatedly appear to you at least four times.[3] It may appear to you at different angles, in different aspects, or as different animals of the same species.

11. After an animal has presented itself to you four times, ask the spirit animal to be your ally, to merge with your being. Imagine yourself embracing the animal, and then return rapidly to ordinary reality. Envision bringing the animal spirit back with you. Your power animal will readily return with you, otherwise it would not have revealed itself. Bring nothing else back with you on this journey. The spirit acting as your guide, however, may or may not accompany you. If not, try to return via the same route that you took to arrive. Upon your return to the entrance, thank your spirit guide, emerge from the opening, and return to your body.

12. Once you have returned to ordinary reality, end your drum journey with four strong beats to signal that the sacred time of focus is ended. If listening to a shamanic drumming recording, you will hear a similar call back signal near the end of the track, followed by a short period of rapid drumming to assist you in refocusing your awareness back to your physical body. If for any reason you want to come back before the call back, just retrace your steps back. Sit quietly for a few moments, and then open your eyes.

It would be advisable to record your journey in a journal as soon as you have returned to ordinary reality. Journeys, like dreams, tend to fade quickly from conscious awareness. Keeping a journal provides a record of your spiritual growth and allows you to reflect upon and better interpret journeys. This process engages the subjective mind and intuitive awareness. In some cases, your journey experiences will be clear and easy to understand. At other times, your journey may be dreamlike and full of symbolism. Interpret such journeys as you would any dream. Look for possible associations related to each symbol or image. Don't overanalyze the journey, for its meaning will become clear at the appropriate time.

Do not stress yourself trying to meet your power animal. It will reveal itself only when it is ready and when you are ready. There is a right time and a right place for everything. Nothing may happen on your first journeys. You may only experience darkness. When this happens, simply try again at a different time. You may have to journey on a number of occasions before connecting with your power animal. Shamanic journeywork is a learned skill that improves with practice. The key is to practice and to establish a long-term relationship with your helping spirits.

Once you meet your power animal, you may discover that it was an animal that you have always been attracted to or had an unusual experience with in the wild. It may turn out to be the spirit that acts as your guide during the journey. Since a spirit animal's power is drawn from their wild and instinctual nature, it's uncommon, however, for domesticated animals such as pets to be power animals. Your power animal will most likely be some kind of mammal, bird, reptile, fish, or amphibian. Spend time with your power animal, asking what lessons it brings. Reflect deeply on its behavior and habits, its strengths and weaknesses and how these might be relevant to your own characteristics or circumstances and the changes you may need to make.

Your power animal may teach you some special ways you can use your drum for your shamanic work that you did not know before. It may even teach you a unique drum beat to summon its presence and power. Remember to thank power animals and seek practical ways to give something of value back to the animal world.

Developing a relationship with power animals

You can develop relationships with power animals based on qualities you would like to have in your life. We also discover through relationship with them that the animal spirits may have very individual and specific teachings for each of us. Similar to the way friendships develop gradually, our relationships with power animals grow and deepen based on repeated interaction and building trust over time. Here are some suggestions for developing a relationship with power animals:

1. Hang pictures of animals around your house or work area.
2. Read books about animals.
3. Observe an animal in nature to learn more about it.

4. Take time every day to meditate and tune into an animal.
5. Put on music and dance to help welcome the energy of a power animal into your body. Embody the power animal and move like it would move.
6. Give gratitude to a power animal whenever it shares a piece of wisdom or supports you in any way.
7. Simply visualize and call upon an animal. When you call or invoke the power of an animal, you are asking to be drawn into complete harmony with the strength of that creature's essence. Meditate with it. Ask what message it has for you. How does it want to be honored? What does it want to tell you?
8. Contemplate what it means if you're not comfortable with a power animal. If you dislike or are afraid of an animal, it's especially important to connect with it and learn its wisdom. The message it holds for you will be particularly meaningful. Power animals help us connect to the parts of ourselves that we've lost or denied, so it may be mirroring a trait or quality that is ready to come back to help you be in your wholeness.
9. Put items on your altar to honor a power animal and represent its energy.
10. Ritually feed and honor helping spirits with offerings such as cornmeal or a "spirit plate" with bits of food placed outdoors at mealtime. Cornmeal is a good offering because corn is a sacred gift from the beings that live in the spirit world. The one offering the cornmeal first breathes on the grains so that the spirits know who is offering the gift.

Chapter 5

Creating Sacred Space

Your sacred space is where you can find yourself over and over again.
—Joseph Campbell

I made my first pilgrimage to the Maya pyramids and ceremonial centers of Mexico in March of 1994. It was an empowering, transformational journey of self-discovery—the culmination of a lifelong dream to explore the pyramidal temples found at Chichen Itza, Uxmal, Palenque and Tulum. Climbing the towering stepped pyramids was a rite of passage for me. Within the vision chambers atop each pyramid, the spirit of the Black Jaguar guided me on underworld journeys of initiation and soul integration. I first learned about these magnificent pyramids in elementary school. When I saw a photo of the imposing Kukulkan Pyramid at Chichen Itza in my world geography textbook, I knew that I had to go there someday, and so I did.

Before I visited the archaeological sites, I learned as much about the Maya as I could. The ancient Maya were very shamanic. To open a path of communication between the spiritual and earthly realms, Maya shamans entered sacred time and space at the top of great pyramids. For the Maya, the establishment of sacred space involved the connecting of the earth with the heavens—to bring them into accord. To rejoin the two separated worlds and regenerate the order of the cosmos, shamans performed rituals to create a portal to the "Otherworld." The sacred, universal space that they created was the center of the heavens and the center of the earth.

From the center of this holy space, the shaman priests and kings brought forth a vibrant energy force that the Maya believe emanates from a divine spiritual source. Shaman kings channeled and directed this life force energy, or *ch'ulel*, through the use of ritual. The ancient Maya kings were called *ch'ul ahaw*, lords of the life force. They used pyramids to bring *ch'ulel* pouring into the universe from the underlying force fields of the Otherworld.

Once brought into the world of humanity, these Otherworld forces and beings could be materialized in ritual objects, in features of the landscape, or in the actual body of a human performer. To reciprocate, the shamans sent maize, incense, and blood offerings through the open portal to nurture and honor the spirits.

The Maya believed that bloodletting was the best way to keep the divine life force circulating. Blood was the primary carrier of *ch'ulel*. Bloodletting was an important ritual of communication. In the rapture of bloodletting rituals, the shaman priests opened a path of communication between the human world and the Otherworld. During the bloodletting rituals, the Vision Serpent, which symbolized the path of communication between the worlds, was seen rising in the clouds of copal incense and smoke above the temple housing the vision chamber. In the vision chamber atop each pyramid, the entranced shaman king and priests communed with the ancestors and with the gods of the Otherworld.

In Maya cosmology, the ongoing creation of the universe occurs through a mutual divine-human interaction; humans are the keepers and co-creators of this reality. They practiced a form of sympathetic magic: the belief that all things mirror each other, so much so that when human beings imitate mythological events in the Dream Time, they reactivate those supernatural events and manifest them on earth. Their ultimate creative goal was ecstatic oneness with the Great Mystery. The highest value of Maya learning was the cultivation of the soul, the process for growing it into a deeper, more durable version of itself than it had been when it had entered this world.

To the Maya, art created reality rather than the other way around. The ancient pyramids and plazas of the Maya ceremonial centers are monumental works of art that replicate in symbolic form the sacred landscape generated by the gods at Creation. The massive stepped pyramids symbolize sacred mountains rising in majestic splendor from a great plaza, representing the primordial ocean of Creation from which all things are arisen. Pyramids, like mountains, are sacred places where heaven and earth meet. Viewed from above, the top of the pyramids makes them the centers of the world; seen from below, they stand against the horizon like World Axes, their steps like a ladder to be climbed. World Mountains are both the center and the axis of the cosmos.

Each pyramid of these ancient geomantic sites is a portal to the spirit world, as well as a powerful generator of life force. The shaman priests arranged the pyramids so that as the night sky wheeled through its yearly cycle to reenact the events of creation, the temples would engage this celestial pattern and reactivate the Dream Time of the first awakening. Replicating the pattern of magnetic power points that dot the surrounding landscape, as well as patterns of stars in the night sky, the temples of Chichen Itza, Uxmal, Palenque and many other major Maya sites form a dynamic matrix of immense power.

Entering sacred space

According to Maya shamanism, the world's center is not located in any one earthly place, but can be materialized through ritual anywhere on earth. We can create sacred space and summon the healing power of spirit anywhere on the planet. To call in the spirits, begin by preparing a purified sacred space where well-being and health can flourish. Sacred space is that territory that we enter for spiritual and inner work. Preparing sacred space shifts our awareness from ordinary waking consciousness to a more centered, meditative state. Ritual preparation awakens our connection to the web of life and structures a boundary that separates the sacred from the ordinary and profane.

There are no rules or restrictions governing this process, although tradition suggests that you begin by smudging. Smudging is the burning of herbs for cleansing, purification, and protection of sacred space. Smudging cleanses the mind and environment by dispelling any stagnant or unwanted energy. Sage, cedar, juniper, and sweetgrass are commonly used for smudging.

To smudge, light the herbs in a fire-resistant receptacle, and then blow out the flames, or burn them on a hot coal or pressed charcoal tablet. When using charcoal tablets, the smudge bowl should be filled with sand or a flat stone to prevent overheating the container. I recommend cracking a window or door for ventilation and for releasing unwanted energies.

Next, use a feather or your hands to draw the smoke over your heart, throat, and face to open the energy channels of your body and raise your personal power or windhorse. According to Mongolian shamanism, windhorse, or *hiimori*, can be increased through smudging, drumming, and other forms of shamanic practice in order to accomplish significant aims.

In Tuva, juniper smoke is sacred and an intricate part of everyday life. Sacred smoke encircles the shaman's patient, family, and yurt or sacred space. It is the smoke of blessing, purifier, prayer sender, and also the extractor of disease. Smoke is also one of the foods for spirits. The spirits eat just as people eat. Tuvan shamans believe that "if the spirits are not fed, the ritual may not go well."[1]

The following is a list of herbs that I use in my shamanic practice. You can use them independently or mix them together in a smudge bowl. Each plant imparts specific qualities when burned. Remember to thank the plant or tree spirit whose body made the cleansing possible. To assist you in creating sacred space:

1. Smudge with the smoke of cedar or juniper for protection, deep cleansing, and the dispelling of negativity.
2. Smudge with white sage or common sagebrush for cleansing, blessing, and for calling in the specific spirits that you require to aid you in the task at hand.
3. Burn sweet grass, the breath of the Earth Mother, to attract and draw in the helping spirits that are called upon.
4. Use copal resin, the blood of trees, to honor the Tree People for providing our first breath, which is spirit, and to call upon the ancestral spirits for their oversight, insight, and protection.
5. Offer tobacco smoke or a pinch of dry tobacco to carry your prayers to the Loom of Creation, thereby reweaving the pattern of existence in accordance with those prayers.

Drum and rattle

Musical sound is widely regarded as one of the most effective ways of creating sacred space and establishing connections with the spirit realm. The drum and rattle are two of the most common musical instruments used to clear and open sacred space. You can create sacred space by describing a circle with the rattle while shaking it. The shaking rattle will break up and disperse any stagnant or unwanted energy. It is also possible to direct energy with rattles, much like a magician with a magic wand. Healing energy can be mentally transmitted through the rattle and out into the environment or into a patient's body. Prayer and intention can be broadcast to the spirit world. Shamans believe that the sound of the rattle opens doors to the spirit world and attracts the attention of its inhabitants. Rattles are a universal, cross-cultural tool for invoking the assistance of power animals and helping spirits.

The drum is also a versatile instrument for creating sacred space. You can use it to summon the spirits into a ritual or ceremony. According to Wallace Black Elk, the renowned Lakota shaman, "When you pray with that drum, when the spirits hear that drum, it echoes. They hear this drum, and they hear your voice loud and clear."[2] Conversely, a forceful beat of the drum can be used to drive away malevolent spirits or intrusive energies that cause confusion, disease, and disharmony. Used in this way, the drum facilitates the creation of a purified sacred space.

Cosmologically, the drum depicts a microcosm of the universe, as well as the vehicle of travel. Carried away on the sound of the drum, the shaman's spirit is said to ride on the animal whose hide is stretched over the drum frame. The frame of the shaman's drum is invariably round, symbolizing the circle of life. In the shaman's world, all aspects of life, energy, and the ever-moving universe spiral in circles. The plants, the animals, the minerals, and the elemental forces of nature all exist within the circle.

The Medicine Wheel of Life

The Medicine Wheel provides another means of entering sacred space and time. The Medicine Wheel of Life is a mandala, a symbolic blueprint or map of reality. It represents a multidimensional, interwoven web of relationships that are in constant communion with each other. The sacred wheel exists simultaneously in a horizontal and vertical axis, as well as in the unfolding continuum of time—past, present, and future.

The Medicine Wheel of Life serves as a portal to consciously enter the cyclic, time-space unfolding of Tao or Great Mystery through a practice of reverent, harmonious relationship. It is based on the belief that the universe is alive, sentient, and constantly communicating its wisdom to who ever makes an effort to listen.

To move around the wheel and develop a relationship with each direction is to step onto a path of learning and fulfillment. Each direction has qualities and attributes that help us spiral toward completion on the wheel of life. All creatures walk the circumference of the Medicine Wheel, experiencing birth, life, and death. After completing a cycle of learning on the sacred wheel, each of us returns to the source, the Great Mystery at the center or heart of the circle.

The Medicine Wheel of Life is symbolized by a circle that is bisected first with a line of light from East to West. From the East the sun arises and the guardian Eagle takes flight. Though the qualities attributed to each of the four cardinal directions tend to vary from culture to culture, the energy of the East is typically associated with the vernal equinox, Eagle, Hummingbird, morning, birth, beginnings, the rising sun, illumination, inspiration, ascending consciousness, and the element of Air.

From the South rises the vital energy of renewal, regeneration, and growth. From the South we learn to plant seeds of good cause. We learn that our thoughts and actions create our reality. South is related to the summer solstice, Serpent, Coyote, midday, youth, trust, growth, and the element of Fire.

From the West flows the energy of transformation. In the West we assimilate our life experiences. Experience is the only baggage we carry with us from this Earth walk. From the West we exit the realm of physical experience and join into vast levels of experience in the spirit worlds of light, or we choose to return and walk again the sacred wheel of life. West is connected to the autumnal equinox, Bear, twilight, introspection, emotions, flow, the moon, death, endings, transformation, and the element of Water.

From the North flows the energy that completes the quartering of the circle. From the North we receive wisdom and clarity of mind. North is linked to the winter solstice, Buffalo, night, wisdom, clarity, patience, renewal, blessings, abundance, and the element of Earth.

The elements associated with the four directions are the building blocks of nature and interact with humans in the creative process. The elements are living energies that change and move as we think, and then take the form of our thoughts. Thought is the tool of the mind that shapes physical reality. Every thought, idea, or image in the mind has form and substance. Everything that we perceive begins with a thought, for it is the blending of thought forms with the elemental rhythms that shape physical reality. It is the consciousness of humanity that holds the present physical form of all that we perceive. It is the mind that determines the destiny of forms. We are mind. Our Earth is mind. We live in a universe of mind. From photons to galaxies, life is conscious intelligent energy that can form itself into any pattern or function.

The compass or circular arrangement of the elements also illustrates the sequence of development in the process of manifestation. Born of the silent emptiness of the center, vibration cycles around the periphery of the circle. Moving from East (Air) to South (Fire) to West (Water) to North (Earth), vibration bonds the elements, and then reverses its rotation toward emptiness to begin the cycle anew. The unmanifest essence of vibration precipitates this bonding sequence in order to manifest a desired form. The energy of vibration is alive and, because it is alive, it seeks ways in which to express or manifest itself. As Ute-Tiwa shaman Joseph Rael concludes in his book, *Being and Vibration*, "Apparently materialization occurs because vibration is seeking to purify the center (heart) of its newly formulated form."[3]

Quartering the circle defines all that is the Great Mystery. We are here on earth to experience and realize the mystery. The vision of that mystery is ever present within each of us. When we still the incessant chatter of the mind, we begin to realize the Sacred Vision. We begin to recognize certain qualities from the four directions that help us evolve on the wheel of life.

Father Sky and Mother Earth together generate the powers of creation. The four directions are the power and life-giving forces of the created. When we begin in the East and turn clockwise, acknowledging the four directions, we align ourselves with the powers that shape our reality. We are also creating a circle—a boundary that separates the sacred from the ordinary and profane. Such a ritual creates a sacred space that can be slipped in and out of at will. By creating a circle, we are also structuring an energy pattern that will contain, focus, and amplify the power generated by drumming. A circle will shape the elemental forces into a powerful current that will spiral upward and downward, uniting heaven and earth. Thus, we synchronize our environment and ourselves to the circle of all that exists.

The World Tree

The World Tree provides another means of entering sacred space. In world mythology, The World Tree is the axis mundi, world axis, or central axis of the cosmos. Images of the World Tree exist in nearly all cultures and represent the world center and/or the connection between heaven and earth. The axis mundi links heaven and earth as well as providing a path between the two. Many ancient cultures incorporate the myth of the World Tree, Tree of Life, or Tree of Knowledge, as it is also known. It is familiar today as the Rod of Asclepius, the symbol of medicine. The staff is the axis itself, and the serpent or serpents are the guardians or guides to the other realm.

According to Maya scholar Kenneth Johnson, the massive pyramidal temples found at Chichen Itza, Uxmal, Palenque, and many other major Maya sites were symbols of the World Tree or *wacah chan* axis, "from which the four directions of time flowed."[4] The Maya believed that the world of human beings was connected to the Otherworld along the *wacah chan* axis which ran through the center of existence. This axis was not located in any one earthly place, but could be materialized through ritual anywhere on earth. Most important, it was materialized in the person of the shaman king, who brought it into existence as he stood enthralled in ecstatic trance atop his pyramid-tree. The shaman opened a path of communication between the spiritual and the earthly planes. The ancestors and helping spirits communed with the shaman through such portals. Ultimately, he became the World Tree so that the world's equilibrium could be maintained.

Modern-day Maya continue to live at the "center of the world." Many Mayan communities have their own world center, which is usually a pagan shrine somewhere in or near the village. Like the ancient pyramids, it serves as a power spot representing the *wacah chan* axis of the world, the sacred tree. Centering the world is thus a way of recreating a spatial order that focuses the spiritual forces of the supernatural within the material forms of the human world, rendering these forces accessible to human need.

World Tree meditation

In order to understand how Maya shamans perceive the cosmos, make use of this simple exercise to enter sacred time. Sacred time, unlike ordinary time, represents the cosmic order. Sacred time coexists with ordinary time. In the material world, temporal time arises from physical processes and is the vehicle of change. In the unseen world, sacred time is the foundation of rhythm and motion. It is the adhesive that holds the universe together. Without it, there would be no Loom of Creation upon which to weave the tapestry of existence. To the Maya, the whole world is generated, organized, and evolving according to the World Tree.

1. First, select a location where you will not be interrupted. It must be a quiet space, at least for the duration of the exercise. Smudge the space and yourself with the smoke of an incense or herb. Among the Maya, copal is traditionally used, but cedar or juniper is acceptable.

2. Stand facing the East, with your feet parallel, about six inches apart, and your toes aimed straight ahead. Your knees should be slightly bent, removing any strain on your lower back.

3. Close your eyes and focus on the breath as it enters the nose and fills your lungs, and then gently exhale any tension you might feel. The Maya believe that the tree provides us our first breath, which is spirit, so offer thanks for this gift of life. Continue breathing with a series of even inhalations and exhalations until you are calm and relaxed.

4. Imagine that you are the World Tree standing at the very navel of the universe. Your roots tap deeply into the underworld, and your crown touches the heavens. Visualize Polaris, the North Star (the star that the earth's axis points toward in the northern sky) directly over your head.

5. Now visualize a spiral of energy ascending out of the earth, moving up your spine, the trunk of your own inner World Tree. This energy is grounding, centering, and abundant. In fact, all possible blessings and abundance come to you as a result of this fiery energy.

6. Now imagine another spiral of energy descending from the heavens above, entering your body through the crown of your head and traveling down your spinal column into the earth. This force embodies higher spiritual knowledge and power. It unites you with the totality of a dynamic, interrelated universe. This is the energy the Classic Maya called *itz*, the "dew of heaven."

7. Visualize these two energetic forces as spirals of white light, one moving from the sky into the earth, the other from the earth into the sky. Together they form a symmetrical double spiral traveling up and down your spine, like the double helix formed by the plus and minus strands of DNA.

8. Now stretch your arms out from your sides so that you stand as a cross-tree at the center of all things. To the Maya, the cross is but a symbol of the four directions, the outstretched arms of the great World Tree, and of the fourfold universe itself. You are that universe.

9. At your right hand, to the South, are gathered all the masculine or yang powers of the cosmos. Since the Maya trace their ancestry through patrilineal descent in the male line, these masculine powers include all

the living members of your family. Maya shamanism teaches us to honor all our relations, so for the moment you must forget about any issues you may have with these people. Love them regardless. Also at your right hand are all the attributes associated with maleness, including your sense of power, authority, and assertiveness.

10. Now focus on your left hand. Here in the North are gathered all the feminine or yin powers of the cosmos. So, whether you are male or female, see all your intimate relations, as well as the actual women who come into your life, on your left hand. Once again, forget about any issues you have with these people, and simply love them.

11. Behind you, in the West, lies the past. Your ancestors and the collective spiritual power of all those who went before you reside in the West. When your own time comes to pass on, you will become part of this vast collective unconscious.

12. In front of you, to the East, lies the future. Your children and the spirits of those yet to come are in the East, for they are part of your future. This is the direction of your spiritual path and destiny.

13. Breathe deeply and contemplate your own World Tree. Become totally open, yielding, and receptive until it becomes part of you. Materialize the World Tree at the heart of the world and help sustain the cosmic order.

Calling the spirits

The opening of sacred space is essentially an invocation, calling in the spiritual energies of the seven directions—East, South, West, North, Above, Below, and Within. Calling the spirits is an ancient shamanic rite that is practiced cross-culturally to access and honor the powers of creation. Inviting their presence, participation, and assistance not only aligns us with their power, but also is a way of giving energy that helps revitalize these primal forces.

Calling in the directions is a spiritual activity in and of itself. The orientation embeds you in the living web of life, yielding greater awareness and perspective. It imparts a comprehensive recollection of the basic experience of being fully human. The ritual grounds you completely into the present moment to begin your day or to begin a specific shamanic practice.

The specific words of your invocation to the spirits do not matter. What matters is that your prayer comes from the heart. You must show the spirit world you have passion and heart. The energy that comes in from the source is directed through our hearts. Your heart must be clear and open in order to receive spirit. You must open the heart, empty the mind, and go deep within.

Make sure you have everything you need before starting. Gather together your ritual items and set up an altar. Although an altar is not essential, it provides us with a focus to pray, meditate, and listen. An altar is any structure upon which we place offerings and sacred objects that have spiritual or cosmological significance. It represents your world center. I use a Navajo rug for my altar. I lay the rug in the center of my sacred space and place a stone, a vessel of water, a lit candle, and a feather upon it to represent the four elements: earth, water, fire, and air. You can also place photos of loved ones on your altar so that they are included in your prayers.

1. To perform this ritual, relax, purify, and center yourself as you would for other spiritual work. When you are ready, begin your invocation. There are no rules or restrictions governing this process. On most occasions, a sacred circle is cast in a sun wise direction, whether in the northern or southern hemispheres. Some people like to start in the direction of the current season—Spring = East, Summer = South, Fall = West, and Winter = North; however, I usually begin by calling the spirits of the East.
2. In a group ritual, I like to have the participants stand in a circle or medicine wheel and face each direction in unison. Use your right hand, or hold a feather in your right hand, to fan smudge offerings to the East. You can also offer a pinch of tobacco or corn meal to each direction. An offering is usually made with the right hand. If you have a rattle, shake it four times to open a portal in the East to the spirit world. Using words, chanting, or song, invite the benevolent spirit powers associated with that direction to participate and assist in the ceremony. Welcome the spirits with an open heart and mind. Some people will whistle or make animal sounds to call in spirit helpers. Trust your instincts and intuition in this process.
3. Pause after calling the spirit helpers of the East and listen for any guidance or wisdom that direction has to share. The spirits will always

respond when you call them. Sound does not just travel out into oblivion. There is a call and then a response. Pay attention to any guidance that comes to you. Communication may enter your awareness as a flash of color in your mind's eye, a visual symbol, a tingling of the spine or an inaudible sound heard deep within your soul. It may be visual, auditory, intuitive, or some combination of these. Sometimes it is just a knowing that your helping spirits and guides are now around you. You may feel energy flowing into your hands, feet, or arms or showering down through your crown. When I channel spirit energy, I often feel chills and goosebumps.

4. Next, pivot around clockwise and repeat the same procedure to summon the spirits of the South, the West, and the North. After that, summon Father Sky above and Mother Earth below. When invoking Father Sky, reach to the heavens; when invoking Mother Earth, reach down and touch the ground where you stand.

5. Finally, face the center of the circle (if you are in a group or in a medicine wheel) and bring your hands to your heart to invite the spirit of Within. Call upon the spirit of divine unity that flows from within the center of your being where the six directions meet. Welcome the gifts of balance, oneness, and connection with all things, for all things are one and all things are related.

6. When you have finished your spiritual work, sacred space must be closed. Follow the same procedure as for the opening, but in reverse order. Begin by thanking the spiritual energies of Within, Mother Earth and Father Sky, and then the North, West, South and East in a counterclockwise movement. Shake your rattle to say farewell to the spirits. As you rattle, give thanks to all your relations for the needs met. The phrase "all my relations" is used at the end of a prayer in many shamanic traditions, for all living things share in the relationships of life on Earth. Express your gratitude to the archetypal elements and helping spirits for being with you and send them off, releasing their energies to the seven directions.

Chapter 6

Shapeshifting

Some are so skilled at drumming, they can duplicate the rhythms of various animals. This is used to facilitate a shapeshifting, an aligning with the archetypal forces represented by the animal.
—Ted Andrews, *Animal Speak*[1]

I recently had some crown work done on my teeth. I always call in a special spirit helper to aid me and the dentist during such procedures. This helping spirit first came to me several years ago during a previous dental procedure.

At the time, I was anxious about the appointment. As I sat in my dentist's waiting room, I calmed and centered myself. I called in my spirit helpers for help and healing. Spirit Bear came immediately. It was not until I sat down in my dentist's chair that Snowy Owl first appeared. Here is what happened:

As I settle into my dentist's chair, I close my eyes. I empty myself to allow spirit to fill me. I become like a hollow bone and go deep within. Snowy Owl glides silently to me on outstretched wings, full of mystery and power. She instills courage, confidence, and a serene calm within me. She quells the impulse to fly in fear.

Snowy Owl bears the silence and numbing cold of the Arctic North. She has a soothing, anesthetic effect upon me. Instilled with her predator vision, I have great awareness of all that is around me. Unbound, I soar into the "blue," high above a vast treeless plain cleansed by a blanket of newly fallen snow.

As my journey transpires, part of my consciousness is still lightly connected to the ordinary reality of my physical surroundings. This is necessary during any shamanic work, not just when visiting your dentist or doctor. One must be aware of what is taking place on both the physical and spiritual planes of our multi-dimensional world. You can then respond accordingly to the dentist or the spirits as the need arises.

I feel safe and nurtured during the entire procedure. My dental work and my spirit journey end after nearly two hours. Before I arise from my euphoric slumber, Snowy Owl reveals herself to me as a goddess. I see long tendrils of windblown hair framing a scintillating face. Her grace, beauty, and form eclipse the boundaries of my perception. She possesses special powers not found in other animals. Nature's forces favor Snowy Owl. She is *wakan* (sacred).

The magic of shapeshifting

One of the best ways to connect with power animals is through the art of shapeshifting. In the shaman's world, animals are kin, which is an ancient belief reflected in mythology and in animism—the belief that non-human entities are spiritual beings. It is a mental world where the seen and the unseen, the material and the spiritual merge. As their helping spirits, the shamans "might use animals, anything that grows," says Osuitok Ipeelee, an esteemed Arctic Inuit sculptor. "It was well known that the animals the shamans controlled had the ability to turn into humans. When a shaman was using his magic he had a real change of personality. When the animals entered into him he'd be chanting loudly; if a shaman was turning into a certain animal, he'd make that animal sound. Once he was filled inside, he'd begin to change; his face and his skin followed."[2]

Shapeshifting is more than just transforming into an animal as is often depicted in shamanic accounts and tales. It is the ability to shift your energies to adapt to the demands and changes of daily life. We all learn which activities, behaviors, and attitudes support or hinder our survival and growth. It is a natural and instinctual ability that we all share. The minimal development of this talent is the ability to mimic. We often mimic for the purpose of learning something or to blend in with our social or physical environment. It implies changing one's pattern of appearance or behavior, rather than just using what you already have. Actors, for example, are known for their ability to take on the characteristics of another person or thing.

A shapeshifter is one who manipulates their aura to access a higher or inner power in order to grow and learn. The human aura is the energy field that surrounds the human body in all directions. All shapeshifting occurs on an energy level. If everything is broadcasting its own energy pattern and if you could match and rebroadcast the same pattern, then you would take on the appearance and qualities of the thing you were matching. The only constraining factor is the degree of belief, connection, and energy. To experience this for yourself, try the following simple exercise:

1. Create sacred space as you would for other spiritual work, dim the lights, and sit comfortably erect in a chair or on the floor.
2. Close your eyes and take a couple of deep breaths.
3. Call upon an animal that you have an affinity with. Visualize and invite this animal spirit to come into your body and consciousness.
4. Meditate with it. Be open to the feelings and sensations of being that animal. It is not uncommon to be and see the animal at the same time.
5. Simply observe whatever happens for a few minutes, and then thank the spirit animal and release it.

Shapeshifting to any degree will help you develop a kinship with your animal relatives. Learning to shift your consciousness, to align with and adapt your energies to power animals, opens your heart and mind to the wisdom and strength of the animal world. You must empty yourself so that spirit can embody you. "Become like a hollow bone," a Lakota elder once advised me in the sweat lodge.[3]

Power animal drumming

Drumming is an excellent way to induce embodiment trance states and facilitate shapeshifting. The shaman uses embodiment trance to bring a helping spirit into his or her physical body to allow that spirit to work through the body to heal other people. When an animal spirit is invoked, there is often an accompanying rhythm that comes through. Shamans frequently use these unique rhythms to summon their helping spirits for the work at hand. As Ted Andrews explains in his book *Animal Speak*, "Some are so skilled at drumming, they can duplicate the rhythms of various animals. There is snake drumming, wolf drumming, hawk drumming—a drumming for every animal. As the rhythm is created it plays upon the metabolism of the individual causing entrainment—the individual's own heart and metabolic rhythm is brought into synchronization with the drum beat. This is used to facilitate a shapeshifting, an aligning with the archetypal forces represented by the animal."[4]

Through drumming, it is possible to co-create a resonant field with a power animal. I recently released the CD *Power Animal Drumming* to help the listener connect with power animals.[5] The spirit calling rhythms on this recording evolved over many years through me and fellow shamanic circle drummers who gained and nurtured enduring personal relationships with helping animal spirits. Each pattern creates a vibratory resonance that allows these spirit helpers to be called forth. The drumbeat is the tuner sound. Each rhythm projects onto the body a supportive resonance or sound pattern to which the body can attune. As one resonates in sync with the rhythm of an animal, energy and awareness are exchanged. To experience this for yourself, try the following exercise for shapeshifting into an eagle:

1. First, do some preliminary research on the eagle, its habits, and behaviors. Become familiar enough with it to be able to clearly visualize it in your mind.
2. When you are ready, create sacred space as you would for other spiritual work. Dim the lights, sit comfortably in a chair or on the floor, and center yourself.
3. The next step is to frame a simple and clear statement of your intentions. Whether asking for help or merely getting acquainted with an animal, one must clearly convey the purpose of invoking them.
4. After clearly stating your intention, begin drumming a slow, steady eagle-beat rhythm, and then gradually build in intensity to a tempo of four to seven beats per second. The ascending tempo will induce a deep embodiment trance state and facilitate the shapeshifting. It may take a few minutes for you to fully synchronize with the eagle-beat— the first spirit calling rhythm I ever learned.
5. As the drumming progresses, vividly imagine with every sense an eagle in front of you. This specific imagery serves as an invitation, literally drawing the animal to you. Mentally review all of its qualities. Eagle symbolizes vision, clarity, and foresight. Eagle is known for his ability to help us open our soul to spirit quests and to soar to great spiritual heights.
6. Now imagine that your body is merging with that of the eagle. Visualize the energy of the eagle awakening within you, with all of its

corresponding abilities. You may feel it, see it, sense it, or simply imagine it. As you focus on it, it will occur. All energy follows thought, and Eagle rules the realm of thought. Allow the change to come slowly. It is not uncommon to be and see the animal simultaneously. Be open to the sensations and feelings of being that animal. Feeling is the most important sensation because you want to imagine what it feels like to be that animal. It helps to mimic the posture, movements, and sounds of the animal you are invoking. The degree of merging is limited by any negative attitudes such as reluctance or doubt. The goal is to merge to the greatest degree possible while still retaining a bit of self-awareness.

7. Finally, separate from the animal by imagining yourself back into your physical body. Do not rush the transformation. Imagine the animal fully and completely outside of you once more. Thank the animal for its power, presence, and assistance. Then allow its image to dissipate.

Be flexible in the above steps. Adapt and experiment with them. Shapeshifting is an expressive art. For it to become truly magical, you must employ your own creative imagination and intuition. This exercise is only a beginning. It will not make you a master shapeshifter. To become a good shapeshifter, you must master the art of observation. You cannot shapeshift to an animal if you do not know its behavior, movements, and characteristics. Begin by watching an animal's behavior and record your observations, your feelings, and your insights. Mimic its postures, movements, and sounds. Imagine what it would be like to be that animal.

The hollow bone teaching

The hollow bone teaching is an ancient practice in Zen Buddhism, shamanism, and Native American spirituality. It is another way to shift your consciousness to become an empty vessel for spirit. The idea is to become like a hollow bone: a conduit for spirit. When we can move our ego and rational mind out of the way to channel the divine power of the universe through us, all healing is possible.

Frank Fools Crow was a venerated Lakota Holy Man who taught that you must become like a hollow bone to be a great healer. He believed that to become a conduit for the source of all creation helps to sustain the order of existence. According to Fools Crow, "We are called to become hollow bones for our people, and anyone else we can help, and we are not supposed to seek power for our personal use and honor. What we bones really become is the pipeline that connects *Wakan Tanka* [Great Mystery], the Helpers and the community together."[6] In his becoming a hollow bone, Fools Crow believed that he went through four stages:

1. First, he called in *Wakan Tanka* to rid himself of anything that would impede him in any way, such as doubt, questions, or reluctance.
2. Then he recognized himself as a clean tube, ready to be filled with hope, possibilities, and anxious to be filled with power.
3. He experienced the power as it comes surging into him.
4. Finally, giving the power away to others, knowing that as he is emptied out, the Higher Powers will keep filling him with even greater power to be given away.

Becoming a hollow bone

The hollow bone teaching has been with us for thousands of years. In traditional teaching, techniques include ways to clear away anything that could possibly clog the bone of our spirit and mind. Meditative practice is an important part of the ongoing task of keeping our insides clean. This form of meditation also facilitates a transcendent state of unity consciousness. One's sense of being a separate individual gives way to an experience of union, not only with other individuals, but also with the entire universe. True shapeshifting means feeling and recognizing our true oneness with everything else.

The benefits of attaining this state of unity consciousness include relaxation, healing, more energy, better memory, greater mental clarity, enhanced creativity, and communion with the resonating web of life. Feelings of peacefulness, timelessness, and spiritual well-being are common, along with a oneness of feeling and purpose with the totality of a dynamic, interrelated universe. When we feel that deep oneness, we are ecstatic. Ecstasy doesn't necessarily mean joy or bliss. It's the feeling of oneness.

This experience of mystical union with the cosmos is said, by many of the world's spiritual traditions, to be the final realization. Consciousness rediscovers its true nature and recognizes itself in all things. Becoming a hollow bone is a simple and effective way to induce this profound state of consciousness. To become a hollow bone, try the following exercise:

1. Create sacred space as you would for other spiritual work. When you are ready, dim the lights and sit comfortably erect in a chair or on the floor.

2. Close your eyes and breathe slowly and deeply seven times. Let your abdomen rise and fall as you breathe. Focus on the breath as it enters the nose and fills your lungs, and then gently exhale any tension you might feel, clearing the energy channels of your body. Release all of your worldly concerns, doubts, and fears, allowing them to drift off on the air of the wind, on the breath of life. Feel yourself relaxing with each breath.

3. When you are fully relaxed, ask the Higher Powers to remove any blockages that prevent you from functioning as a hollow bone. Repeat the affirmation, "I choose to be a clean, hollow bone." Visualize yourself as a hollow bone or tube that is all shiny on the inside and empty. The cleaner the bone, the more energy you can channel through it, and the faster it will flow.

4. Now begin drumming a slow heartbeat rhythm, and then gradually build in intensity to a tempo of four to seven beats per second. Reversing this and moving from the frenzied drumming to the regular heart rhythm will draw your consciousness back to normal. Focus your attention on the sound of the drum, thereby stilling the chatter in your mind. Allow the drum to empty you. Become one with the drum. Remember that drumming opens portals to the spirit world, draws spirit in, and opens you up to receive it.

5. As you drum, imagine the unifying spirit of the divine source flowing through you. Visualize a spiral of energy descending from the heavens above, entering your hollow bone and traveling down into the earth. You may feel it, see it, sense it, or simply imagine it. As you focus on it, it will occur, for energy and life force follow thought. Allow spirit to flow into and embody you so that the speed and rhythm of your playing come under its control. As Tuvan shaman Sailyk-ool Kanchyyp-ool describes it, "I am not myself. But, I am being maneuvered by the spirits. They tell me. 'Beat hard, beat fast, beat a long beat.' And they also tell me when to stop."[7]

6. As the drum journey evolves, you will become more ecstatic and spirit will perhaps create new rhythms. You are now moving into a higher state of unity consciousness and developing a new shamanic skill. At the higher levels, a healer becomes adept at detaching all sense of self,

being fully present in the moment as a hollow bone or living conduit for healing energy to move through.

7. When it feels appropriate, gradually slow the tempo of your drumming to the regular heart rhythm to draw your consciousness back into your body. Do not rush the transformation. Visualize yourself fully grounded in your body, and then slowly open your eyes.

As you will find, the effects of becoming a conduit for the source of all creation are seldom subtle. Expect sometimes dramatic physical responses and emotional releases. We tend to impede the flow of this vital energy, thereby depleting our personal power. Negative attitudes, fear, and envy are mind-sets that constrict the energy channels in the body.

Drumming quickens our frequencies so that we actually begin to spin off the slower vibrations of anger, doubt, and fear. The energy channels of the body are cleared as we move into an ecstatic state of harmonic resonance with the primordial essence of being. By becoming a conductor of divine knowing energy, we can access the invisible sea of information that we bathe in daily, the all-pervading frequencies of consciousness immanent in all phenomena.

Tuvan shamans mostly work with this spiritual energy in their healing and rituals. Known as *küsh*, it is the force that a shaman invokes from the earth and sky. They believe that the sky or heavenly *küsh* falls only on the drum: not on other things or people. One cannot catch a cosmic signal without drumming. According to Tuvan ethnographer and poet Mongush Kenin-Lopsan, "The drum provides the common signal that puts to work the heavenly power with the shaman. When sky signals come down, they look like invisible fire, or fire rays. When a shaman calls and gets these heavenly powers, the people present at the ceremony feel differently. They faint or they laugh, or cry, or they are happy. They experience different feelings."[8]

When playing a drum, life force energy flows between the drumhead and the drumstick. With practice, you should be able to feel this subtle force pushing and pulling on the drumstick. This pure source energy is divine will or intention to be. As Cherokee wisdom-keeper Dhyani Ywahoo puts it, "Will is the underlying current, the fire that brings forth that which we perceive as our reality."[9] If you allow this force to guide your drumming, you will begin to flow along the current of will. You will be in accord with will, the voice of the original source, the fundamental sound underlying all manifestation. Thus you become an instrument of creation in the material world.

Power animal attributes

By following the steps outlined in the preceding exercise, you can practice shapeshifting into any power animal you feel an affinity with. You can become a hollow bone and imagine the spirit of a specific animal flowing through you with all of its corresponding qualities and abilities. Channeling a spirit animal will assist you in attuning to and manifesting the attributes you desire from it. An exchange of energy and awareness takes place between you and the spirit you channel. They have much to share if you listen with your heart. Shapeshifting will help you develop a kinship with your animal relatives and the ability to invoke their power for the benefit of the community.

Keep in mind that animal spirits choose to come into relationship with the person seeking. You can seek power animals, but the spirits must choose. I have seen people seek power animals, yet never get chosen.

Below you will find a brief dictionary of power animal symbolism. Power animal traits reflect human characteristics. By learning the nature of an animal, you can also look at what part of your nature is most like that of the animal. Remember to thank power animals and seek practical ways to give something of value back to the animal world. Power animal attributes are as follows:

Badger medicine includes courage, cunning, endurance, grounding, perseverance, root and herbal remedies, and the magic of storytelling. Badger is a very aggressive and utterly fearless fighter. Invoke Badger for courage, fighting spirit, and persistence. From her den below the ground, Badger connects us to the Earth Mother, her stories, and the healing properties of medicinal roots. Badger helps us see below the surface of things and boldly express ourselves with the clarity of inner knowing.

Bear qualities include introspection, solitude, intuition, healing, courage, strength, security, grounding, determination, dreams, and transformation. Bear symbolizes feminine energies, hibernating to reconnect with the earth each winter, and then emerging each spring with answers to spiritual dilemmas. Spirit Bear is known to many cultures as the "great healer." The task of the great healer is to cure disease and restore harmony and balance. Invoke Spirit Bear to heal mental, physical, and spiritual wounds and to absorb all the emotional and physical toxins within you.

Beaver represents determination, diligence, dreams, intuition, work, accomplishment, structure, flexibility, security, family, and enjoyment. Beaver is an ingenious builder who can dam the flow of an entire river. Beaver medicine is akin to earth and water energy. Earth is open, loving, nurturing, and the giver of form to all matter. Water symbolizes our intuition and dreams. Invoke Beaver to help you structure your life so that you can joyously manifest your dreams and strengthen your relationships with friends and family.

Buffalo/Bison symbolizes prayer, manifestation, and abundance. Buffalo's medicine includes creativity, feminine courage, abundance, knowledge, generosity, hospitality, sharing work, protection, strength, challenge, survival, and giving for the greater good. Buffalo teaches us the importance of prayer and gratitude for all we have. In Lakota Native American spirituality, *Tatanka*, the Buffalo, is seen as a living prayer and manifestation of the wisdom and generosity of *Wakan Tanka*. To manifest abundance through prayer, you must eliminate all doubt, detach yourself from the outcome, and trust in the creative power of the universe to provide what is needed.

Butterfly is an ancient symbol of magic, transmutation, and the never-ending cycle of transformation. Virtually all cultures have marveled at the magical process that transforms an ungraceful caterpillar into a magnificent fluttering Butterfly. To use Butterfly medicine, you must determine your position in the cycle of self-transformation. Like Butterfly, you are always at a certain station in your life activities. You may be at the egg stage, which is the beginning of all things. This is the stage at which an idea is born, but has not yet become a reality. To bring an intended pattern into being, you must make a clean sweep of negative, limiting, or otherwise outmoded patterns, and then start anew. The larva stage is the point at which you decide to create the idea in the physical world. The cocoon stage involves going within: doing or developing your idea or project. The final stage of transformation or transmutation is the leaving of the chrysalis and birth. The last step involves sharing the colors and joy of your creation with the world.

Coyote is a cunning shapeshifter who can adapt to any habitat. While the habitats of most predators are diminishing, Coyote's territory is expanding. Call upon Coyote for these shapeshifting qualities, but beware, for Coyote is a magician, trickster, and heyoka. The heyoka or sacred clown uses satire, folly, and misadventure to awaken people to innovative and better ways of doing things. Sometimes we unwittingly cut off the voice of our inner truth, or sense of what is correct, relying instead on old, soul-killing patterns of judgment, control, and distrust. Inner truth reflects, like a mirror, the higher, universal truth that exists in every situation. Yet even when our point of view is at its most positional, narrow, and self-righteous, higher truth, often in the guise of the trickster, is there to open the way back to balance and wholeness.

Crow is sociable, curious, adaptable, resourceful, skillful, playful, magical, and a mythological trickster or heyoka. The heyoka behaves in ways that are contrary to conventional norms in order to startle and awaken society to innovative and progressive ways of doing things. Crow's lesson is to stop acting out of habit. You must be willing to plow old habits into the soil in order to cultivate new patterns that enhance your natural growth. Innovative change will revitalize your life and precipitate renewed growth and creativity. Invoke Crow for magical powers, for shapeshifting abilities, and for the bold expression of your inner vision.

Deer symbolizes gentleness, alertness, speed, adaptability, and the healing power of love and generosity. Deer is a magical creature that leads us into the transcendent realm of the collective unconscious, the infinite creative matrix of all that we are and have ever been. Deer hoof rattles are associated with thunder, and the antlers of the buck represent antenna, which attune us to the spirit world and awaken new psychic gifts. In the physical realm, Deer reminds us to be alert and pay attention before we leap into action. Deer medicine instills an understanding of what's truly necessary for survival and what to sacrifice for the higher good. Deer teaches us to find the gentleness of spirit that heals all wounds. We must be gentle with ourselves, in spite of our errors, and gentle with others who react from a place of fear or anger.

Dragon is a mythical creature that continues to exist in another dimension. Dragon medicine represents wisdom, illumination, protection, magic, vitality, inspiration, shapeshifting, transformation, and the inner knowing of the true self. Dragon's power is that of shedding its skin and coming out as a new, transformed being. Dragon transmutes with the mastery of the infinite self, bringing us to the culmination of our multi-dimensional existence. Invoke dragon to help you fulfill your own unique path of self-realization. As always, trust your inner voice.

Eagle symbolizes strength, vision, clarity, and foresight. Eagle medicine is the ability to soar above the hurdles of life's dilemmas, keeping one's attention focused on more distant horizons of self-realization. Eagle reminds us to pay attention to what really matters in life. Eagle Brother/First Shaman, like the drum, carries our prayers to the Higher Powers. Eagle will enable you to fly higher or just go deeper within yourself. Many shamans call upon Eagle to help them develop their shamanic powers.

Elephant medicine includes dignity, grace, strength, wisdom, confidence, patience, commitment, gentleness, discernment, intelligence, compassion, collective memory, and removal of obstacles. In the Eastern traditions, the Elephant's head denotes wisdom, and its trunk represents OM, the primal sound from which the universe constantly emanates. Tribal peoples invoke Elephant for health, good luck, longevity, and the insight of collective memory. Elephant connects us to the wisdom of the collective unconscious, the common psychological inheritance of humanity.

Elk medicine includes stamina, strength, cadence, confidence, empowerment, sensual passion, and the inspirational power and influence of sound energy. As the days shorten and temperatures drop in autumn, bull Elk use sound to attract mates. Sound is regarded as one of the most powerful ways of establishing connections. Elk shows us how to use sound to inspire others, stirring them into action. We gain the confidence to fully express our ideas and intentions in an inspirational manner. Elk teaches us how to reclaim our power and how to pace ourselves to reach our goals.

Flicker is a woodpecker, whose thrumming is commonly associated with drumming and rhythm. Flicker is a master drummer that can link you to any other rhythm in the universe. All things are born of rhythm and it is rhythm that holds them in form. Rhythm is the heartbeat of life. Every living thing has a unique song, a pulsing rhythm that belongs only to it. Within the heart of each of us, there exists a silent pulse of perfect rhythm that connects us to the totality of a rhythmic, interrelated universe. The resonating circle of life will remain unbroken as long as each individual retains his or her own rhythm, while allowing others to do the same.

Frog symbolizes rain, cleansing, purification, healing, renewal, transformation, and magic. Their magic is reflected in their metamorphosis from aqueous tadpoles to air-breathing creatures which can live on land. It is this kinship to the element of water that gives Frog medicine great cleansing and healing properties. In knowing the element of water, Frog can use its drum-like ribbit to invoke the Thunder Beings—thunder, lightning, wind, and rain—to cleanse and replenish the earth with water. Frog teaches us how to recognize when it is time to purify our bodies and our environments so that healing can occur on all levels. Connecting with Frog energy provides the opportunity to purify, refresh, and replenish the soul.

Grouse is an archetype of rhythm, sacred dance, and the cosmic spiral. The spiral represents the rhythmic movement of life force energy. The male Ruffed Grouse dances in a stylized spiral during courtship and produces a drumming sound by a rhythmic beating of the wings. Rhythmic movement is energy that creates change. The male Grouse signals a time of new rhythms and movement by drumming the air with rapidly beating wings, releasing the energy to the four directions. Working with new rhythms and movements will open the flow of life force into your life.

Hawk is a visionary, protector, and messenger of the air. Like the shaman, Hawk is an intercessor between the physical and spiritual worlds. Hawk moves gracefully between the earth and sky, joining both realms together. Hawks and owls possess the keenest eyesight of all raptors, giving them broad vision. Hawk feathers and energies are used in Pueblo ceremonies for calling the Thunder Beings to bring the rains and sustain the earth. Hawk's shrill call can awaken us from our spiritual amnesia, shatter our self-created illusions, and realign us with the original intention of our soul. Invoke Hawk to help you rediscover your core values and purpose for being here.

Horse represents personal power, stamina, endurance, freedom, independence, travel, adventure, and soul flight. "Horse is a medicine or you could say a relationship with the spirit of Horse such that the Horse will let you (your spirit) ride him and will take you where you want to go."[10] The driving beat of shamanic drumming is suggestive of a Horse on a journey. Mongolian shamans describe it as the exalted, buoyant state that one mounts and rides through the inner realms of consciousness. The wild, untamed spirit of Horse will teach you how to ride the drum into vast worlds of extraordinary richness and complexity.

Hummingbird is associated with joy, love, magic, endurance, and luck. This tiny iridescent bird is a dynamo of energy, darting tirelessly from flower to flower in search of nectar. Hummingbirds can teach us how to use flowers for healing and to win hearts in love. The playful Hummingbird sings a vibration of pure joy and shows us how to find happiness in all things. Invoke Hummingbird to help you find joy and sweetness in any situation.

Jaguar represents shamanic power, magic, shapeshifting, transformation, and the life-and-death principle. She embodies the wisdom of the underworld, the primal space of the unconscious deep within each of us. Jaguar's lesson is to move beyond your fear of the dark unknown. Jaguar is the epitome of a chaotic storm moving through your life, all the while demanding you to remain calm, centered, and grounded. This fierce animal is the gatekeeper to the unknowable. Jaguar medicine includes comprehending the patterns of chaos, walking without fear in the darkness, moving in unknown places, soul work, and reclaiming power. Invoke Jaguar to reclaim your true power.

Mourning Dove is maternal, gentle, serene, and embodies peace, love, and harmony. She is linked with dawn and dusk, when the veil between the seen and unseen worlds is at its thinnest. Dove can help us connect with the spirit world at these times. The Mourning Dove's song speaks to our heart and stirs our emotions. Its mournful coo soothes our soul and calms our troubled thoughts, allowing us to find renewal in the silence of mind. Dove teaches us that, regardless of external circumstances, peace is always within us. We need only still the mind and go within.

Osprey is a messenger, guide, psychopomp, fearless protector of its young, and guardian of both the air (consciousness) and the water (the unconscious) it dives into for fish. Like the shaman, Osprey moves between the seen and unseen realms, joining both worlds together. Osprey is a master shapeshifter who merges light and darkness, seeing both inner and outer reality. Invoke Osprey to help you integrate conscious and unconscious awareness, thereby renewing the flow of intuitive mind. Intuition reveals appropriate action in the moment for a given set of circumstances. Synchronous activity appears within consciousness as the most natural thing to do. One can readily perceive what aims are in accord with the cosmos and not waste energy on discordant pursuits. So long as one follows one's intuitive sense, one's actions will be in sync with the true self and ultimately the cosmos.

Owl medicine includes prophecy, wisdom, stealth, silence, intuition, clairvoyance, clairaudience, shapeshifting, and keen vision that can pierce all illusion. Call upon Owl to unmask and see what is truly beneath the surface—what is hidden or in the shadows. Night Eagle, as Owl is called, is the bird of magic and darkness, of prophecy and wisdom. Owls have a large repertoire of haunting calls that can be heard over several miles on a still night. Owl is a messenger of omens who will call out to let all share in its vision.

Polar Bear medicine includes introspection, healing, purity, courage, strength, solitude, spirit flight, dreams, death-and-rebirth, transformation, mystics, and visionaries. On a spiritual level, the Polar Bear is regarded as the embodiment of the spirit of the North, a fearless animal who possesses ancient wisdom and shamanic powers. Japanese and Siberian shamans believe Polar Bear to be the leader of the animals, the animal that taught humans shamanism. Inuit peoples regard Polar Bears as shamans and holy beings. The "flying bear" could take the Inuit shaman to the moon, or deep into the sea to seek help for his people.

Raven represents shamanic power, healing, shapeshifting, self-knowledge, death-and-rebirth, and magic. Raven magic is the ability to let go of the past and change your life—death-and-rebirth. Acquiring shamanic power involves letting go of the self, dispensing with self-dialogue, getting out of the way, and letting the universe do the talking. Among indigenous cultures of the Pacific Northwest Coast, Raven is a messenger of the Great Mystery and a carrier of powerful medicine. Raven carries the power and healing of ritual magic to the intended destination. Invoke Raven to be the courier of your prayers in remote or distant healing.

Red Deer is a magical creature that symbolizes spirit flight, shapeshifting, and the qualities of swiftness, grace, and keen scent. The Red Deer's call is a deep bellowing roar-like-sound similar to a lion's roar. Mongolian shamans revere Red Deer as their distant ancestors and spirit helpers. Red Deer Stag represents the harnessed steed of the shaman in the spirit world—the drum used to induce ecstatic trance.

Salmon symbolizes sustenance, regeneration, fluidity, purpose, resolve, integrity, and the flow of life. The Salmon is an amazing creature that can grow up to four feet in length and weigh over sixty pounds. It has remarkable navigation skills. Salmon finds its way from the sea to the river of its birth and swims upstream overcoming great obstacles to reach its spawning grounds. Salmon are masters of water, which is related to the emotions and change. Salmon teaches us how to overcome obstacles and flow with the shifting waters of change.

Snake medicine represents cosmic consciousness, lightning, creation, fertility, sexuality, reproduction, transmutation, and the all-consuming cycles of death-and-rebirth, exemplified by the shedding of Snake's skin. The ancient Maya invoked serpent deities who dwelled beneath their pyramids. The Vision Serpent was seen rising in the clouds of copal incense and smoke above the vision chamber of the pyramid and symbolized communion with the world of the ancestors and the gods. The Feathered Serpent was a prominent deity of spiritual enlightenment found in many Mesoamerican religions. In the Eastern traditions, a storehouse of fiery energy known as Kundalini, or the Serpent Fire, lies coiled at the base of the spine. When awakened, the Serpent Fire rises up the spine, activating spiritual energy centers and opening new levels of awareness. Invoke Snake to awaken your powers of creativity and inner vision.

Thunder Beings are a related family of divine beings who bring about weather changes such as thunder, lightning, wind, and rain. Through their power abiding in the atmosphere, they sustain the earth and protect the people. Their medicine includes creativity, fertility, growth, protection, death-and-rebirth, peace, harmony, balance, compassion, wisdom, and enlightenment. From time immemorial, people have worshiped the Thunder Beings. In the Oriental traditions, they are responsible for originating or expressing the higher truth of spiritual reality, safeguarding it, and disseminating it for the benefit of all beings. The early cultures and their belief systems were initiated by Thunder Beings. "The Thunder-beings known as Wandjina originated Australian shamanic tradition. The Thunder-beings known as Tengeri originated Mongolian shamanic tradition. The Thunder-beings known as Tunkashila, Animiki, and Kachinas originated Native American traditions."[11] They are the roots of all integral wisdom traditions. We can relate to them in storms, but primarily we must seek them within. The drum can help us in this quest for it embodies the spirit and quickening energy of the Thunder Beings. Horse hide is often used for "thunderer" drums because it is widely associated with Thunder Beings and creates a voice that carries a long way.

Turtle is nurturing, grounding, receptive, protective, patient, enduring, adaptable, tenacious, and self-reliant. Turtle is an ancient symbol for the earth. She is the personification of goddess energy and the Earth Mother herself. Many Native Americans refer to North America as Turtle Island because when the earth was once covered with water, Turtle journeyed to the bottom of the ocean, bringing earth up on its back so that animals and people could have a home. Turtle asks us to honor and respect the reciprocal cycle of give and take. Be mindful of returning to the earth what she has given you. Mother Earth provides everything we need to live and flourish. Express your gratitude through prayer and offerings.

Chapter 7

Shamanic Music

The dungur [drum] plays music for the spirits, and for the shaman's spirit to find the spirits.
—Kara-Ool, Tuvan shaman[1]

I love to ski and shamanize. I recently spent two weeks camping and cross-country skiing in the mountains of sunny Central Oregon. The spring skiing is usually excellent at the Mt. Bachelor Nordic Ski Center. I camp most nights a few miles below the Nordic center at the Virginia Miessner Nordic Sno-Park. Meissner is a great place to camp because the ample parking area is often free of snow and has vault toilets, along with a thirty-foot diameter warming yurt where I improvise shamanic music. I sleep like a monk in a mummy bag on an air mattress inside a fiberglass canopy mounted on the back of my pickup.

Each morning, I arise early to greet the sun with song and prayers. I then cook a simple meal of oatmeal with dried cranberries, chopped almonds, and green tea. After breakfast, I am ready to begin shamanic skiing—my offering to all our relations. As I kick and glide along the groomed trails, I sing songs to the forest and mountain spirits. I sing to the plants, birds, and animals. I pause to touch and connect with the elder mountain hemlocks along the trail. I thank them for the oxygen that I breathe and send out prayers of gratitude to the Tree of Life. I thank the Thunder Beings for sending down a glorious white blanket of snow to totally neutralize the harmful causes of disease.

On my final morning of skiing, Thunder Beings arise in the sky and adorn themselves in dark clouds over nearby Newberry Volcano. As I return to the Nordic lodge, the Thunder Beings speak through a clap of rolling thunder. It resonates to my very core. Nothing heightens my senses like the voice of the Thunder Beings. Whenever I hear the rumbling thunder, I take a moment to acknowledge and thank these divine beings for the work they do and the blessings they bestow upon the earth. The Thunder Beings are the force behind all weather changes and sustain life on earth. Through lightning, they directly purify the air we breathe, the water we drink, and the earth we cultivate. I make an offering of tobacco and supplicate the Thunder Beings to bestow their enlightenment upon us as the lightning enlightens the earth.

After sunset, as I do each evening, I enter the nearby yurt and begin another round of shamanizing. I open portals to the spirit world with drum, rattle, and flute. I call in the Thunder Beings and improvise an evening of shamanic music. I approach them with humbleness and humility, becoming like a hollow bone through which their life force may flow to be used as needed, then returned to the Sky Father. Alone in a mountain yurt, I offer myself as a vehicle of healing. That is how I choose to relate to the spirit world.

At the end, after dedicating the power that has been generated by the performance, I close the circle. I then crawl into my sleeping bag, physically tired, yet spiritually vibrant. My heart is wide open and blissful. I love reconnecting with the spirits in the dynamic volcanic mountains where my shamanic journey began so many years ago.

Shamanism and music

Shamanism and music combined thousands of years ago. By observing nature, shamans perceived that the power of sound could be used to help and heal others. The first drums and musical instruments were put to shamanic use, as were many of the early singing traditions. According to folklorist Kira Van Deusen, "In a shaman's world music operates in several ways. It helps the shaman and other participants in a ceremony to locate and enter the inner world, opening the inner, spiritual ear and eye. Musical sound calls helping spirits and transports the shaman on the journey. Both the rhythm and the timbre of musical sound help heal the patient through the effects of specific frequencies and musical styles on the human body."[2]

Shamanic music is traditionally performed as part of a shamanic ritual; however, it is not a musical performance in the normal sense. According to Scottish percussionist Ken Hyder, who has studied with Siberian shamans, "musical considerations are minimal in shamanic performance." The shaman's focus is on the spiritual intention or the energy of what is being played. When the performer concentrates on the spiritual aspect of playing, it allows the music to become very loose, spontaneous, and innovative. Hyder explains, "My approach to music making changed decisively following my experiences in Siberia. For me it starts with the dungur [drum] and the expanded possibilities of variation arising from its superficially apparent instability. And it continues to open up with other musicians being equally free in themselves and in the context of a group. That opening up has the capacity to expand and expand further making the playing fresh, different and spontaneous each time."[3]

Shamanic music is improvised by the shaman to modify movement and change while actively journeying into the spirit world. It is a musical expression of the soul, supporting the shamanic flight of the soul. Sacred music is directed more to the spirit world than to an audience. The shaman's attention is directed inwards towards communication with the spirits, rather than outwards to any listeners who might be present.

Another way that the shaman expresses their experiences in the spirit world is through their physical movements in this reality. In their journeys, shamans are often flying, running, crouching, stalking and fighting unseen spirits. All of these movements are acted out for all to see in a shamanic performance.

A shaman uses various ways of making sounds to communicate with the spirits, as well as relate the tone and content of the inner trance experience in real time. Shamans may chant, clap their hands, imitate the sounds of birds and animals, or play various instruments. Of particular importance are the shaman's drum and song.

Each shaman has his or her own song. It announces the shaman to the spirits and proclaims, "this is me … please help me." The song is usually sung near the beginning of the ritual and is often accompanied by drumming. Singing brings the heartbeat and body into resonance with the song similar to entrainment with the pulse of the drum. As the shaman's song invokes the intended spirits, the shaman comes into resonance with these spirit energies as well.

Finding your power song

Power songs are oral prayers spoken from the heart, expressing your true self and personal power. I recommend that you find your own power song to invoke your spirit helpers. The lyrics are usually just a line or two repeated over and over. The words of your song will have great power if they come from the heart. As ethnographer and author Gregory Maskarinec puts it, "In the shamanic world, words transform substance. Any medicinal properties of raw substance are trivial compared with the power of speech ...."[4]

To acquire a power song, begin your day with morning prayers to your helping spirits. Ask your guides to help you discover your personal power song. Do not eat breakfast and fast throughout the day. Plan to spend the day alone in an outdoor location that is preferably quiet and private. A wilderness or wild area away from the city is preferred.

Do not plan an itinerary—be spontaneous. Just stroll quietly through the natural setting with the awareness that communication with natural elements is possible and be open to such communication. Nature is communicating with you all the time. Be aware of your surroundings. Look for synchronicities. They involve an internal psychological event that corresponds to an external observable event. Some aspect of a journey, vision, or dream may manifest in your ordinary reality. An animal, bird, or insect may bring you a message or guidance. When any animal shows up in an unusual way, or repetitively in a short period of time, it's critical to pay attention to the message. As you wander, discover what animal or bird you feel like. Take on its feelings, embody its spirit, and enjoy its identity throughout the day.

As this is your first attempt to acquire a power song, you may only find the melody. If so, subsequent excursions will unveil the words for your melody. Until you find your own song, I give you the words of one that I found shortly after beginning my shamanic training:

Oh spirits awaken with light,
On wings of the Eagle take flight.
Soar between the Earth and Sky,
And in harmony unite with me.

From the Lower World you arise,
To bring me power and advise.
Ride the winds of the World's Rim,
Then descend to me at the Center.

When invoking your spirit helpers, repeat the song as long as you feel it is needed. I often start dancing and rattling while I sing my power song and bring my whole body into the act of calling the spirits. The more feeling or emotional energy you put into it, the stronger the invocation.

Music and its role in ritual

Music is an essential tool in shamanic ritual and healing work. Music is used to contain the energetic or spiritual aspect of the sacred space, which is defined physically by the assembled people who participate. Dance and song propel the ritual process forward by providing a vehicle for self-expression within the sacred space. Together the musicians create the necessary container that channels the energy generated by the performance in ways that the shaman can guide toward the ritual's intended outcome.

Three elements are constantly interacting in communal healing rites: the shaman who guides the flow and pattern of the ritual, the musicians who contain the sacred space, and the gathered people who participate. Interaction between all three elements is necessary to maintain the energy, flow, and intention of the ritual.

Music is also used to crack open the part of the self that holds emotions in check. For example, in funeral rites among the Dagara people of West Africa, drumming and singing are used to open the mourners to grief. Grief is then channeled in such a way that it will convey the newly deceased soul to the afterlife. Without the help of the drummers, musicians, and singers, the powerful emotional energy cannot be unleashed. If not channeled properly, grief is useless to the dead and dangerous to the living. According to Christina Pratt, author of *An Encyclopedia of Shamanism*, "This musical container of the ritual space must be maintained continuously. The musicians do not rest as long as the ritual continues, though the ritual may last one to four full days."[5]

Auditory illusion

Shamans are also known for their ability to create unusual auditory phenomena. Percussionist Ken Hyder explains, "Shamans tend to move around a lot when they are playing, so a listener will hear a lot of changes in the sound ... including a mini-Doppler effect. And if the shaman is singing at the same time, the voice will also change as its vibration plays on the drumhead."[6]

Furthermore, in a recent ethnographic study of Chukchi shamans, it was found that in a confined space, shamans are capable of directing the sound of their voice and drum to different parts of the room. The sounds appear to shift around the room, seemingly on their own. Shamans accomplish this through the use of standing waves, an acoustic phenomenon produced by the interference between sound waves as they reflect between walls. Sound waves either combine or cancel, causing certain resonant frequencies to either intensify or completely disappear. Sound becomes distorted and seems to expand and move about the room as the shaman performs. Moreover, sound can appear to emanate from both outside and inside the body of the listener, a sensation which anthropologists claimed, "could be distinctly uncomfortable and unnerving."[7]

Sending out a sound

Sound is regarded as one of the most effective ways of establishing connections with the spirit realm, since it travels through space, permeates visual and physical barriers, and conveys information from the unseen world. Sound, therefore, is a means of "relationship" as well as a "transformation" of energy.

Sound does not just travel out into oblivion. There is a call and then a response. When Iroquoian people of present-day central and upstate New York discuss "sending out a sound," they mention blowing on a conch shell and using the turtle rattle to attract attention, signaling the start of a ceremony, notifying the community, and drawing the Creator's participation.[8] The conch is sounded at the beginning of important rituals because the sound is believed to have the ability to drown out any negative words or noises that might disturb or disrupt the harmonious atmosphere. The sound of the conch is understood as the source of all existence—a cosmic womb, for when the conch is blown, it is said to emulate the primordial sound from which all else emanates.

According to the Haudenosaunee (Iroquois), when the turtle rattle is shaken, "the earth stops to listen." The turtle rattle is a symbol of the world on the turtle's back, Turtle Island. The Creator is said to have loved snapping turtle best. When Mother Earth hears the sound of the turtle rattle, all of creation awakens and moves to its shaking beat. The crack of a turtle rattle, which shakes the earth, draws the attention of the spirits at the beginning of a ceremony or meeting. "To Shake the Earth" is a metaphor often used in Iroquoian communities to describe the purpose of the turtle rattle.[9]

The Drum

Sacred music is based on a simple trio of instruments: the drum, the rattle, and the flute. The sound of the shaman's drum is very important. A shamanic ritual often begins with heating the drum head over a fire to bring it up to the desired pitch. Shamans may strike certain parts of the drum to summon particular helping spirits. It is the subtle variations in timbre and ever-changing overtones of the drum that allow the shaman to communicate with the spiritual realm. The shaman uses the drum to create a bridge to the spirit world, while simultaneously opening the awareness of all the participants to that bridge.

All elements of drum music such as timbre, rhythm, volume, and tempo play an important role in shamanic ritual. By using different parts of the drumstick to play on different parts of the drum, different timbres can be produced for transmitting different meanings. Different rhythms transmit different meanings and enable the shaman to contact different beings in different realms of the cosmos. Volume and tempo arouse feelings in the listener and communicate symbolic meanings directly as aural sense experience.

A shaman may have a repertoire of established rhythms or improvise a new rhythm, uniquely indicated for the situation. The drumming is not re-stricted to a regular tempo, but may pause, speed up, or slow down with irregular accents. The shaman may stop playing altogether, or suddenly hoist the drum skyward and bang it violently, throwing the disease into the heavens and returning it to the spirit world.

The Rattle

Rattles are used to invoke the assistance of power animals and helping spirits. The shaman's rattle draws the spirit world and its inhabitants into the material world, whereas the drum carries the shaman into the spirit world. Hence, rattles and drums work well together. I often use a drum-stick rattle, which is simply a beater with a rawhide rattle attached to the base of the handle opposite the head. When used as a drumstick, the clicking of the rattle adds not only an interesting sound effect, but also produces an offbeat that adds a new dimension to the sonic experience.

The repetitive sound of the rattle, like that of the drum, helps induce trance states. The shaking of rattles creates high-pitched frequencies that complement the low frequencies of drumbeats. The high tones of rattles resonate in the upper parts of the body and head. The low tones of drums act primarily on the abdomen, chest, and organs of balance, while stimulating an impulse toward movement. Rattles stimulate higher frequency nerve pathways in the cerebral cortex than do drums. This higher frequency input supplements the low frequency drumbeats, thereby boosting the total sonic effect.

It is also possible to direct energy with rattles, much like a magician with a magic wand. Healing energy can be mentally transmitted through the rattle and out into the environment or into a patient's body. Prayer and intention can be broadcast to the spirit world. Moreover, you can create sacred space by describing a circle with the rattle while shaking it.

Among Iroquois medicine societies, turtle rattles are described as hands of the spirit beings, and the gourd rattle is described as the sound of Creation. The Iroquoian creation stories tell of the first sound, a shimmering sound, which went out in all directions; this was the sound of "the Creator's thoughts." The seeds of the gourd rattle embody the voice of the Creator, since they are the source of newly created life. The seeds within the rattle scatter the illusions of the conscious mind, planting seeds of pure and clear mind.

In South America, the shaman's rattle is a most sacred instrument. The rattle is believed to embody the sacred forces of the cosmos through its sounds, structural features, contents, and connection to shamanic trance. The various parts of the rattle also symbolize the structures of the world. The handle is the vertical axis that ascends into the Celestial Realm. The Upper World is represented by the rattle's great head-gourd, which contains spirits. Joining the head of the rattle to the handle symbolizes the joining of masculine and feminine elements in the universe, an act of fertilization that gives the sound of the instrument creative shamanic power. From a shamanic perspective, caretaking the rattle and playing it properly during ritual fulfills the destiny of the human spirit—to sustain the order of existence.

The Flute

According to Ute-Tiwa shaman Joseph Rael, "The flute is an instrument connecting the two worlds, the non-physical with the physical. The breath of the flutist is the breath of God coming through a hollow reed; the sound is that of the invisible lover courting the visible lover, the metaphor of the lover and the beloved."[10]

The flute opens a path of communication between the spiritual and earthly realms. The flute is related to the soul, which extends far beyond the physical body, connecting us to the symphony of the universe. Something transcendent happens when you begin to play a flute. You journey deep inside yourself and bring out the cosmic music of your soul. Nothing matters—audience, place, time—you just get lost in the music. You become the music—notes, rhythm, and melody.

The flute is akin to the breath, which is spirit. Its sound is like the wind, which is dispersive, changeable and unpredictable, yet it has the capacity to permeate anything. The flute is also akin to the birds and flight. Its chirp, warble, and bird-like notes make your heart soar. The flute is like the air; you cannot hold it or contain it, and yet you can never separate yourself from it. "Everything needs the air and so the flute represents the voice of the soul and the voice of the wind, and the voice of the birds—those things that are free, free to move. So taken all together this trio, the flute, drum and rattle, represents the whole voice of Creation."[11]

Chapter 8

Shamanic Drumming

My drum can connect me to the earth or carry me like a flying horse. Sometimes I send my spirits out, but other times I must go myself, alone or with the spirits.
—Tania Kobezhikova, Khakass shaman[1]

The repetitive, rhythmic cadence of shamanic drumming is evocative of a horse on a journey. Mongolian shamans describe it as the buoyant, transcendent state that one mounts and rides from plane to plane. We can ride Spirit Horse on journeys through the inner realms of consciousness or call upon Horse to be the courier of our prayers in remote or distant healing.

I first rode Spirit Horse in 1989 at my first shamanic drumming circle in Sedona, Arizona. That drum journey transformed my life. Four years later, Spirit Horse transformed me once again. Here is what happened:

Jade Wah'oo Grigori, my mentor and teacher, stood before me. "Find Spirit Horse," he exclaimed! The shaman vanished from my dreams as quickly as he had appeared. I awoke in the morning with the words "find Spirit Horse" indelibly etched in my mind. I had not seen or spoken to Jade in over four years, but I remembered full well his teachings of Spirit Horse. Jade had taught me that, through shamanic drumming, one could ride Spirit Horse for personal empowerment and healing the land.

I contemplated this dream throughout the day, trying to discern its meaning. I was finally drawn to a stack of *Shaman's Drum* magazines in my office. I fervently leafed through the magazines with no idea of what I was looking for. Midway through the stack, I opened the winter 1990-91 issue to an article titled "Native Americans Join Efforts to Preserve Sacred Ridge on Mount Hood."

Enola Hill, a densely forested, pristine watershed ridge on Mount Hood (Oregon), was under the threat of logging operations. A coalition of

Native Americans, historians, and environmentalists appealed and delayed the U.S. Forest Service's timber sale, pending ethnographic studies to determine the area's cultural significance. The ethnographic studies revealed that Enola Hill is a *tawyash*, a Sahaptin Indian word for a place where spiritual power can be obtained and maintained. For thousands of years, Enola has been a Native American Mecca—a revered and sacred place for pilgrimages, ceremonies, and vision quests.

As I continued to read the article, I came across a reference to a spectacular waterfall known to the indigenous people as Spirit Horse Falls (Devil Falls on USDA maps). The falls got its name from vision questers who saw a Spirit Horse rising from the mist. As I read these words, I was overcome by a profound sense of euphoria and resolve. I knew that this sacred waterfall was the Spirit Horse that Jade had told me to find. I expressed my gratitude for this gift in a prayer to Great Mystery.

Two weeks later, I stood for the first time on Enola Hill, overlooking Spirit Horse Falls. The sound of the thundering falls and the sublime beauty of the temperate rainforest filled my senses with a lucid-like awareness. I felt a holistic connection to my Earth Mother. In my heart I felt that I had finally come home. I drummed and performed a ritual for the protection and preservation of this sacred place that provided spiritual power for this region. I prayed that this nerve center in the web of life would continue to distribute vital energy throughout the surrounding natural systems.

Afterwards, I made the three-hour drive back to my home in Bend, Oregon. That night, and for many nights to follow, my dreams were filled with drums, Enola Hill, and Spirit Horse Falls. Four days after drumming on Enola Hill, I undertook the following journey:

My spirit soared over the forested slopes of the Cascade Mountains to Mount Hood and Enola Hill. I walked up Enola Hill toward Spirit Horse Falls. I reached the falls and stepped into the cascading torrent of icy cold water. My spirit merged with that of the water. I felt the rushing water carry me down into a cavern deep within the earth. My awareness separated from the water and catapulted upward out of the cavern to a moss covered boulder at the base of the falls. I rested on the boulder, gazing up at the roaring falls. I detected a glow emanating from the falls—red, orange, yellow—all the colors of the rainbow. A rainbow arched in the mist above the falls.

A spirit horse emerged from the mist. A scintillating black horse, followed by a luminous red horse, followed by a brilliant yellow horse, and finally a radiant white horse. The horses circled and pranced in the mist. They approached and circled me. I stood at the center.

"I am from the west," said the black horse. "I come to you to protect this sacred waterfall. Call upon the sacred power of the west when you pray and I will come."

I climbed onto the black horse and rode it west to the Pacific Ocean, and then returned to the falls. I dismounted and hovered in the mist above the falls.

The red horse approached. I mounted it and rode east toward the rising sun. We entered the sun and it turned red. The horse burst out of the sun, leaving a luminescent vapor trail in its wake. A sunbeam transported us back to the falls.

From the south came the yellow horse. I mounted it and rode south. A warm glow emanated from the horse, casting a yellow light on the landscape around us. I rode, holding onto the mane, gathering power from the south. We arrived in Chichen Itza, Mexico. The horse carried me to the top of the Kukulkan Pyramid. A brilliant star descended to the pyramid. We merged with the essence of the star.

"Take my power back to the waterfall," commanded the star. "Take the power of the pyramids back to the waterfall!"

The horse bolted from the star, streaming a trail of yellow light behind it. Iridescent orbs of light followed closely behind, playfully oscillating to and fro. The yellow horse delivered me to the falls, and then dissolved into the mist along with the orbs of light.

The radiant white horse of wisdom came forth. I climbed on and it whisked me skyward to the north. I held tightly onto its mane as it circled high above Mount Hood.

"Drum around this sacred volcano," advised the white horse. "Drum at Spirit Horse Falls. Call upon the power of the four horses to bring protection and healing power to this sacred place."

The white horse guided me to other waterfalls around the mountain.

"Drum also at Wallalute, Sahale, and Tamanawas Falls," urged the horse. "This you must do. You will drum the waterfalls around this mountain. Always begin your journey at Spirit Horse Falls and find Spirit Horse. Drum around this sacred mountain."

The white horse carried me to the top of Mount Hood. I gazed down upon the surrounding meadows and forest. The landscape was luminous and vibrant with energy.

"Drum around this sacred mountain of light," the horse continued. "Learn from the sacred places. This is your work. Drum the falls of Mount Hood. Consecrate them. Awaken them. Bring the drum and prayers. This is the place of awakening. Always begin at the falls. Make that pilgrimage."

Looking below, I could see lines of light linking all the waterfalls and sacred places. A network of energy lines formed a complex web that linked together all life forms.

"Drum at all the sacred waterfalls around the mountain," said the horse. "I will show you where they are. The rivers that flow from this mountain are sacred. These rivers feed the spirit. This water will awaken the people when you drum at the falls. All who touch this water will be awakened. Drum the sacred waters!"

"Where will I live," I asked?

"Near this place of power," the horse replied. "A home will be provided from which you will go out to drum the sacred places. When you are finished here, you will move on. It is time to consecrate these sacred places. The time has come to awaken them."

The white horse galloped down the mountain to Enola Hill and Spirit Horse Falls. I dismounted and stood upon the rainbow that arched above the falls. The white horse returned to the north. The yellow horse returned to the south. The black horse returned to the west, and the red horse to the east. I stood at the center. My awareness merged again with the waterfall to be swept into the cavern deep within the earth. I then ascended to the falls and returned to my body.

The preceding journey was particularly powerful and a revelation to me. The journey revealed to me that I could be of greatest service to my Earth Mother at Spirit Horse Falls. Three months after taking this journey, a friend contacted me regarding a year-long, live-in caretaker position in the Mount Hood area. Elisia and I soon relocated to a community near Enola Hill and Spirit Horse Falls. We spent much of the summer hiking to waterfalls and drumming the sacred waters. By the end of the summer, we had completed a circuit around Mount Hood. Having completed our mission, we felt the inner urge to move on. We returned to Bend, Oregon, yet Spirit Horse Falls will always be a significant power place for me. I still make pilgrimages to the falls to pray and drum.

The shaman's horse

The shaman's horse, namely the single-headed frame drum, originated in Siberia, together with shamanism itself thousands of years ago. Shamanic drumming is considered one of the oldest methods for healing and accessing inner wisdom. Practiced cross-culturally, this technique is strikingly similar the world over. Shamanic drumming uses a single, repetitive rhythm played at a tempo of three to four beats per second. Although sounding quite simple and redundant, the unique connection between the drum and the shaman gives this drumming great power, richness, and depth.

According to Tuvan musicologist Valentina Suzukei, "shamanic drumming is not monotonous at all. Constant changes in timbre and volume keep them interesting. The healing quality lies in this variation, which tracks and directs the patient's energies. If you don't listen for timbre, but only for pitch and rhythm the music is boring, monotonous. But the player's every smallest change of mood is reflected in timbre."[2]

Through the many frequencies and overtones of the drum, the shaman communes with the normally unseen energies of the spirit world. By changing and listening to the tones, pitches, and harmonics of the drum, the shaman is able to send messages to—and receive them from—both the spirit world and the patient.

The shamanic drum is a time-tested vehicle for healing and self-expression. A shaman may use the drum to address any number of health issues including trauma, addiction, depression, and chronic pain. Additionally, the shamanic techniques of extraction, soul retrieval, and journeying, can all be performed with the drum. According to Mariko Namba Walter and Eva Jane Neumann Fridman, authors of *Shamanism: An Encyclopedia of World Beliefs, Practices, and Culture*, "The drum is used in a variety of ways in shamanist rituals; it may serve as (1) a rhythm instrument, (2) a divination table, (3) a "speaker" for communicating with the spirits, (4) a spirit-catcher, (5) a spirit boat, (6) a purifying device, (7) the shaman's mount."[3]

What is shamanic drumming?

Basically, shamanic drumming is a technique of accessing and directing archetypal or transpersonal powers for healing and manifesting what is needed to benefit the community. It is a simple and effortless way to still the incessant chatter of the mind, thereby inducing a shamanic trance state.

Shamanic drumming carries awareness into the transcendent realm of the collective unconscious, the infinite creative matrix of all that we are and have ever been. It is an inward spiritual journey of ecstasy in which one interacts with the inner world, thereby influencing the outer world.

The following exercise is designed to acquaint you with the process of shamanic drumming. Allow yourself up to thirty minutes for this exercise. To perform the exercise, you will need a drum. If you do not have a drum, simply improvise one from available materials. Try tapping on an overturned plastic container with a spoon. Keep in mind that the larger the container, the deeper the sound. A five-gallon bucket, for example, makes an excellent improvised drum. Read through the exercise first to familiarize yourself with the process.

The potential is unlimited, yet the fundamentals of shamanic drumming are relatively simple. The basic steps that I find most effective are as follows:

1. Create sacred space as you would for other spiritual work and invoke the spiritual energies of the seven directions—East, South, West, North, Above, Below, and Within. When you are ready, dim the lights and sit comfortably erect in a chair or on the floor.
2. The next step is to calm and focus your mind by performing a simple concentration exercise. Close your eyes and focus on the breath as it enters the nose and fills your lungs, and then gently exhale any tension you might feel. Continue breathing with a series of even inhalations and exhalations until you are calm and relaxed.
3. Once you are fully relaxed, it is important to form your intention: what you desire or expect to accomplish. Intent is a kind of decision making that directs the focus of our attention. It is through our attention that we influence and direct the aspects of our experience and the world

around us. Those aspects of our experience that are most enduring are the effect of habitual expectations and beliefs. What we pay attention to becomes what we know as ourselves and our world, for energy flows where attention goes. As Mihaly Csikszentmihalyi points out in *Flow: The Psychology of Optimal Experience*, "We create ourselves by how we invest this energy. Memories, thoughts, and feelings are all shaped by how we use it. And it is an energy under our control, hence, attention is our most important tool in the task of improving the quality of experience."[4] The greater the clarity and focus, the greater the effect.

Sustained focused attention on a specific intention, while in a state of inner silence, allows your intent to penetrate the Upper World, the inner plane of consciousness where the original patterns or blueprints for all things exist. Such attention channels the infinite energy of the universe into manifesting the physical equivalent of the focus. You can focus your intention on anything. Your conscious intent could be to help or heal yourself, someone else, or the planet. You may wish to manifest something or to influence events in the material world. You could ask for the power to manifest your full potential, talents, and purpose, or simply ask for whatever guidance or knowledge you need at this time. Be mindful, however, of the motives underlying your intent. Intentions motivated by malice, greed, envy, and the like are seldom fruitful and will only block your spiritual growth.

To clarify what it is you truly need, it is helpful to word your intention in a concise and clear-cut manner. You must be specific about what you desire, for you will receive exactly what you ask for. Reciting a descriptive word or phrase aloud will help sustain your focus as well as provide a clear pattern which the power of the universe can express into manifestation. It is important to affirm your intention with belief and expectation. You must eliminate all doubt and trust the creative power of your intent. The keynote of intent is that all you will ever need exists as potential and is waiting to manifest.

4. Having formed your intention, commence the first or "prayer" round of drumming. If you happen to have a double-headed drum, always begin on the Upper World or higher-pitched side of the drum. A steady, metronome-like rhythm pulsed at around three to four beats per second is the most effective. A rapid eagle-beat evokes the sensation of inner movement, which, if you allow it, will carry you along. It is

projective in nature and carries your intention, prayers, and awareness into the heavenly archetypal realm. It is best to stroke the drum firmly, yet gently, producing ringing tones and overtones. Move the drumstick around the drumhead as you play. If you can, find the drum's sweet spot, that place where the drum begins to talk, hum, and sing. Work the drum to build up the hum of the overtones. These are the best frequencies for healing and raising windhorse or personal power. The whole drum needs to sing.

5. As you drum, repeat the word or phrase that represents your intent over and over like a mantra. Reciting a mantra directly into the drum charges it with energy and informs the drum's spirit of your intention. Sustain your focus until you sense intuitively that your intention has penetrated the matrix of archetypal patterns that shape and direct our reality. There are several key indicators that confirm you have connected to the Celestial Realm and seeded the blueprint of the desired outcome. The sound of the drum tends to change. The drum's pitch, timbre, or volume may appear to rise or fall. Another indication is a change in resonance. The hum of the ringing overtones tends to intensify with a crescendo, gradually increasing in volume until a climactic connection is made and then subsiding. With practice, you will learn to sense such subtle indicators. Part of the shaman's training involves learning to receive and interpret a larger range of frequencies than the normal person can.

6. Once you have introduced your intention, begin the second or "healing" round by drumming a slow heartbeat rhythm, and then gradually build in intensity to a tempo of about three to four beats per second. This healing pulse is magnetic and receptive in nature, drawing awareness, archetypal knowledge, and transpersonal powers down into the material world. It empowers and gives form to the pattern of your intent. The heartbeat also draws the energy of the original cosmological pattern down into the earthly realm, helping to align you and the web of life with the original intention for the earth. If using a double-headed drum, play the Lower World or lower-pitched side of the drum. Sustain the heartbeat rhythm for as long as you feel it is appropriate. It is best to trust your intuition in this process. Each person must ultimately go within to find their own internal timing.

7. As you drum, clear your mind of everything. Give up the need for control. Paradoxically, focused intent, to be effective, must be followed by

complete surrender and detachment. You must relinquish completely both the specifics of your goal and how that goal is to be achieved. The unknowable powers of the universe will create what is needed, often in a most unpredictable way. You must be confident that the outcome, while out of your own hands, is in the process of being changed or created. This requires an attitude of surrender and trust.

8. Close your eyes and focus on the sound of the drum, keeping your mind open to insights. Don't worry about missing a beat or falling out of rhythm. Allow yourself to be swept along with the rhythm. If your mind wanders, bring the focus of your attention back to the beat of the drum. Stay aware of what you are experiencing without trying to analyze or question its meaning. Simply observe the thoughts and ideas as they flow in and out of awareness. Insight and guidance regarding your original intention may come through visions, symbols, or images. It may simply be an intuitive, knowing awareness. You might witness a symbolic or dramatic presentation, which offers insight into your situation. You may be led on a journey to a landscape and meet a helping spirit who tells you what you want to know. Accept whatever happens with humility and grace.

9. If you are in need of healing or are healing someone else, then merely let the drum do the healing. Become like a hollow bone, and allow the spirit of your drum to embody you so that your playing comes under its control. When embodying spirits, they will actually dictate the rhythm and speed until you reach something that is suitable for them. The drum's spirit will generate, access, and direct healing energy based solely on your original intention.

10. When you feel the power ebbing, begin the final or "thank you" round of drumming. Drum once again the even cadence of the eagle-beat. Play the Upper World or higher-pitched side of a double-headed drum. Sustain a steady pulse of three to four beats per second for several minutes. As you drum, give thanks to all your relations for the needs met. The drum will propel your gratitude into the archetypal realm. Give thanks also for the needs you are asking to be manifested. Giving thanks before needs are met is a way of making space to receive them. Expressing gratitude for something before it actually appears in your life develops trust and confidence in your ability to create. The creative power of your intent is limited only by what you believe is possible.

11. Finally, end your drumming with four strong beats to signal that the sacred time of focus is ended. When you have finished your spiritual work, sacred space must be closed. Follow the same procedure as for the opening, but in reverse order. Begin by thanking the spiritual energies of Within, Mother Earth, Father Sky, and then the North, the West, the South and the East in a counterclockwise movement.

I have found these fundamentals of shamanic drumming to be very effective in a myriad of situations. Feel free, however, to adapt them to serve your own needs. Rhythm is a very personal thing. Experiment with different tempos and improvise new rhythms.

Rhythm healing

The key to understanding the shaman's world is to realize that the universe is made of vibrational energy: that it is a single, flowing, rhythmic being. According to quantum physics, everything in the universe, from the smallest subatomic particle to the largest star, has an inherent vibrational pattern. The entire universe is created through vibration and can be influenced through the vibrations of shamanic drumming. The shaman's drum is a tool for altering the vibrational state of the shaman and/or the patient or a particular situation in the community. Shamanic drumming is an ancient form of rhythm healing.

Rhythm healing is an approach that uses therapeutic rhythm techniques to promote health and well-being. Rhythm healing employs specialized rhythmic drumming patterns designed to influence the internal rhythmic patterns of the individual and harmonize those which are thought to be causing the illness or imbalance. When administered correctly, specific rhythms may be used to accelerate physical healing, stimulate the release of emotional trauma, and produce deeper self-awareness. This technique has been used for thousands of years by indigenous cultures around the planet to treat a variety of conditions.

In Manchu shamanic drumming, for example, rhythmic patterns with odd accents are frequently used, which are related to the cosmology of Manchu shamanism in which the cosmos has nine levels divided into three regions. As ethnomusicologist Lisha Li points out, "before healing a patient, the shaman beats his drum very hard three times, then chants and beats the drum repeatedly in three-fold rhythms."[5] According to old

Manchu shamans, "Three-accented Patterns" are for accessing the Celestial Realm, "Five-accented Patterns" are for conveying the intention of spirits to the people, "Seven-accented Patterns" are used to drive away malevolent spirits, and "Nine-accented Patterns" are for working with all living beings in different regions of the cosmos.

Rhythm healing relies on the natural laws of resonance and entrainment to restore the vibrational integrity of body, mind, and spirit. In resonance, the sound waves produced by the drum impart their energy to the resonating systems of the body, mind, and spirit, making them vibrate in sympathy. When we drum, our living flesh, brainwaves, and spiritual energy centers begin to vibrate in response. According to percussionist Dru Kristel, this sympathetic resonance "leaves reverberating effects up to 48 to 72 hours after a session."[6] A single-headed frame or hoop drum works best for rhythm healing—the larger the drum, the greater the resonance.

Entrainment occurs when two or more frequencies come into step or in phase with each other. For example, if two pendulums swinging at different rates are placed next to each other, they will gradually entrain until they are locked in perfect synchronization. They entrain because it requires less energy to pulse in unison than in opposition. Nature always seeks the most efficient energy state. The body's electromagnetic auric field, together with internal rhythms such as heartbeat and brain waves, will also entrain with the drum's rhythm.

Though the rhythm healer may have a repertoire of established rhythms, every situation is unique. Determining the right rhythm in each case is a highly individual matter. No predetermined formulas are given. The rhythmist needs to create a dialogue between the sounds he/she produces and the responses of the person being treated.

Tuvan shamans, for example, often improvise sounds, rhythms, and chants in order to converse with both the spirit world and the patient. The sounds produced by the shaman and the drum go out and certain frequencies and overtones are then reflected back. Information is generally received as subtle vibrations, which the shaman then interprets as sounds, pictures, or as rhythms.

Tuvan ethnographer and shaman Mongush Kenin-Lopsan describes the healing effects of the drum, "The speed and strength of the drum strokes depend on the nature of the ailment. The drum sound acts as a signal from the sky, provoking a voice from the cosmos. In turn the instrument is necessary to catch these signals."[7]

Through trained observation, the rhythm healer discovers the right rhythm for their patient. It may be a new rhythm, uniquely indicated for the situation. This means that one must learn to listen very carefully to the sound of the drum. The drum, like all our relations, is alive and trying to tell you something. Listen with more than just your ears.

To hear the voice of the drum, you must listen with your entire being. Ask your drum and your helping spirits to help you. State your intention in a clear and concise manner, and then let go of the self. You must open the heart, empty the mind, and go deep within. Become like a hollow bone, and allow the spirits to flow through you. Give up the need for control. This requires an attitude of surrender and trust.

I learned that when I trust my spirit helpers to play the appropriate rhythm, which I don't know in advance, I can't go wrong. I know only that what I play is what I experience, and it is a way to honor my helping spirits. I also feel a profound connection with everything around me. The key is to let spirit work through you for the purpose of healing—to become an instrument of healing.

Rhythm healing is about transposing already existing harmonics into sound by stroking them from the drum. Rhythm and resonance order the natural world. Dissonance and disharmony arise only when we limit our capacity to resonate totally and completely with the rhythms of life. The origin of the word rhythm is Greek meaning "to flow." We can learn to flow with the rhythms of life by simply learning to feel the beat or pulse while drumming. It is a way of bringing the essential self into accord with the flow of a dynamic, interrelated universe, helping us feel connected rather than isolated and estranged.

Every rhythm has its own quality and touches you in a unique way. These qualities, in fact, exist within each of us, longing to be activated. It is this process of internalization that allows us to access the inaudible yet perceptible soul, so to speak, of a rhythm. Another paradox of rhythm is that the audible pattern is the inverse of the "inaudible matrix." Every rhythm has both an inaudible and audible aspect—silence and sound. It is the inaudible intervals between audible beats, which allow us to hear the grouping of beats in a coherent cycle or pattern. We sense the interval as the off-beat or light element and the audible beat as the heavy element. The drummer establishes the audible beat, whereas the silent pulse quality unfolds by itself in any rhythmic pattern.

In rhythm healing, the drumbeat is the tuner sound—the sound that fuses the silent and audible aspects of vibration into one resonance. The drum pattern projects onto the body a supportive resonance or sound pattern to which the body can attune. This sympathetic resonance forms new harmonic alignments, opens the body's various energy meridians and chakras, releases blocked emotional patterns, promotes healing, and helps reconnect us to our core, enhancing our sense of empowerment and stimulating our creative expression.

Divination

Divination is another way to determine the appropriate rhythm for a particular situation. Divination is the art of seeing and interpreting signs in everything around us. The goal of shamanic divination is to encourage well-being by helping a person live in harmony with the universe around them. One of the best known systems of divination is the I Ching, or Book of Changes. Consulting the I Ching is one of the best ways that I know to restore harmony wherever there is disharmony. Restoring harmony is the primary work of the shaman.

The wisdom unveiled in the I Ching is simple and consistent: if we relate correctly, keeping ourselves in harmony with the universe, all things work out beneficially for all concerned. The I Ching reflects the philosophy that all events, past, present and future are part of a single, interrelated whole. It describes the universe as a vast rhythmic entity and all things in it in constant cyclical change. The central theme is that all things move in predictable patterns or cycles, therefore no situation is static or immutable.

The I Ching is a codebook of archetypal patterns in which the hexagrams counsel appropriate action in the moment for a given set of circumstances. Each moment has a pattern to it, and everything that happens in that moment is interconnected. Based on the synchronicity of the universe and the laws of probability, the I Ching responds to an inquiry in the form of a hexagram. By evaluating the hexagram that describes your current pattern of relationship, you can divine the outcome and act accordingly. The oracle serves as a gauge—a precise means for placing oneself in relation to the pattern or way of cyclical change, and that way is known as Tao.

As a system of divination, the I Ching reflects your current connection with Tao. It serves to freeze the present moment at the time of your inquiry, responding in the form of a hexagram. By evaluating the hexagram that describes your current pattern of relationship, you can divine the outcome and act accordingly. The pattern integrity of the "Canon of Change" has remained intact for thousands of years.

The I Ching is a microcosm of all possible human situations. It serves as a dynamic map, whose function is to reveal one's relative position in the cosmos of events. The hexagram texts address the sixty-four archetypal human situations. The commentary of each hexagram reveals the optimal strategy for integrating or harmonizing with the inevitable for a given condition. It provides the appropriate response to your inquiry. It affords a holistic perspective of your current condition and discusses the proper or correct way to address the situation.

More importantly, the pattern image of each hexagram depicts a particular drum pattern, which renders the essence of each hexagram into sound, thereby allowing the drummer to attune to the resonances that are affecting his/her situation. A solid yang line _____ represents one whole beat, while a broken yin line __ __ represents two half beats or a heartbeat. The rhythmic pattern of Hexagram 58 - Joy, for example, resembles the opening beats of the familiar processional "The Wedding March." This simple drum pattern is depicted below. All I Ching linear image patterns are read or played from bottom to top.

Line 6	__ __	drum—drum	in white
Line 5	_____	drum	dressed
Line 4	_____	drum	all
Line 3	__ __	drum—drum	the bride
Line 2	_____	drum	comes
Line 1	_____	drum	Here

Drumming the appropriate hexagram rhythm creates a vibratory resonance that stimulates, works with, and informs the body, mind, and spirit in the most optimal manner for integrating or harmonizing with the inevitable for the given condition. The drummer then embodies the qualities necessary to effect change or harmonize with change. These qualities will be engendered in you and resonate out to influence all aspects of your experience. The lower trigram resonates its qualities within the body, while the upper trigram resonates without, thereby bringing the inner and outer aspects of the self into accord with the situation, state, or condition.

Consulting the I Ching

To consult the I Ching, one must first frame an inquiry. Formulating an appropriate question and writing it down is a key element in the process of divination. Focusing on a question develops a receptive state of mind and helps you clarify what it is you are truly seeking. It is important to word your inquiry in a concise and clear-cut manner. A vague question will elicit an ambiguous or misleading response. Appropriate inquiries might be worded as follows:

1. "Which hexagram(s) am I to work with today?"
2. "Which hexagram(s) best describe my present situation?"
3. "Which hexagram(s) should I drum at this time in order to harmonize my body, mind, and spirit?"
4. "Which hexagram(s) should I drum at this time in order to heal my illness?"

Drumming the hexagram

Remember that each hexagram is read or played from bottom to top. While drumming a hexagram, you should have a receptive attitude of calm, positive expectation. Such resonant receptivity allows whatever factors or forces are present to fully penetrate your senses. Any attempt to analyze or conceptualize the experience will only fragment the resonant field, obstructing your connection. Follow your inner sense of timing as to both the tempo and time span to drum. Trust your internal timing. It connects you to the resonances affecting your situation. The key is to still the mind, and focus your attention on the hexagram image.

As the drumming progresses and your inner image of the hexagram becomes clearer, close your eyes and feel yourself being carried away by the rhythm, as if going on a journey into yourself. With time and patience, the rhythm archetype will begin to release a rush of intuitive ideas. Inspiration and insight regarding the situation may flow into your awareness. However, it is not essential that you become cognizant or consciously aware of any particular insight or guidance. Simply resonate in sync with the vibrational pattern that collectively describes or reflects your current condition or connection to Tao. The inherent resonant qualities will interpenetrate every aspect of your being.

After drumming the hexagram, repose in the sonic afterglow. When the final drumbeat fades into silence, an inaudible, yet perceptible pulsation persists for a brief period. Sense this silent pulse resonating within your body. You may experience the sensation of every particle in your body pulsing in sync with the rhythm you just played. This synchrony of inner pulse with the appropriate hexagram rhythm brings you into accord with the conditions and forces governing or affecting your inquiry. More information on hexagram drumming can be found in my book *I Ching: The Tao of Drumming.*[8]

Drum divination

The drum can be utilized as a divination tool. The Sámi peoples of northern Scandinavia and the Kola Peninsula in Russia were renowned for their drum divination skills. They used divination to determine the future, luck or misfortune, location of game, diagnosis, and remedies. The Sámi practiced an indigenous form of shamanism until the religious repression of shamanic practices in the mid 17th century. The *runebomme*, an oval frame or bowl drum, was an important trance and divination tool of the *noaidi*, or Sámi shaman. The reindeer, which was central to Sámi culture and livelihood, provided the hide for the drumhead, the sinew to lace it together, and the antler bone for the drumstick or hammer. The Sámi believed that the reindeer's antlers were conduits to the Upper World.

Sámi drumheads are decorated with cosmological rune symbols and drawings of heavenly bodies, plants, animals, humans, and human habitations, sometimes divided into separate regions by horizontal or vertical lines. The cover art of this book is a rendering of one of the few remaining 300-year-old Sámi drums.[9] Sámi drums are characterized by a central sun cross with arms protruding in the four cardinal directions. The cross symbolized the sun—the source of life. "The terminal of the lower arm is often embellished, in many cases with a sort of (cave?) opening. This is, according to old descriptions, the starting position for the brass ring or antler piece placed on the drumskin when used for divination. The only other figures commonly found on this arm are the holy day men. These three figures (sometimes just one or two) are usually the most simplified of all human figures, frequently represented by simple crosses."[10]

For divination, the drum is held horizontally with the drum face or table parallel to the floor. A metal ring or other kind of pointer is centered on

118

the top of the drumhead. The drum is gently played with the drumstick so that the pointer moves across the drumhead, but does not fall to the floor. The diviner observes the movement of the pointer in relation to the symbols on the drum to interpret the answer. Detailed instructions on how to make and use divination drums can be found in Richard Webster's book *Oghams & Oracles: Divination in the Druidic Tradition.*[11]

Working with your shamanic drum

From a shamanic perspective, drums are living beings, helping spirits, and allies. They deserve the utmost in honor, respect, and care. For this reason, one should always "drum the beat" rather than "beat the drum." Venting your frustrations by pounding on a drum is not recommended. It is not necessary to strike the drum sharply to bring out its unique voice and resonance. That is not to say that one cannot play the drum with passion and abandon. It is best to stroke the drum firmly, yet gently, producing ringing tones and overtones. Use short strokes with a minimal amount of motion to pull the sound out of the drum. Keep your arms and shoulders relaxed, breathing slowly and deeply as you play. By playing the drum in this manner, you will have greater precision and endurance.

Move the drumstick around the head of the drum as you play, allowing the various tones and overtones to resonate through you. You will find the higher tones around the edges of the drumhead and the deeper sounds toward the center of the drum. If you can, find the sweet spot—that place where the drum begins to hum and sing. The drum has to sing in order to reach its full potential for healing and empowerment.

Always begin a drumming session by softly stroking the drum, and then gradually increase the intensity of your playing. It is much better to awaken a drum's spirit gently and softly. Imagine someone yelling loudly to awaken you from a deep sleep.

Drumming, for me, is a sacred and profound experience. When I pick up a drum, it is a sacred act. I do so with reverence and respect. I never touch someone else's drum without their permission, and I am very particular about whom I allow to touch or play one of my own. Most people may find such behavior odd and eccentric, but as you develop a relationship with a personal drum, you may begin to share my point of view.

For me, it is important to reserve particular drums for "sacred" work and to set aside others for "social" purposes. I smudge each of my drums periodically as a way of honoring its spirit and to remove any stagnant or unwanted energy. Keep in mind that when you play a drum, it will resonate with other drums in your home. When you play one drum, you are in effect playing all the drums within the proximity of its resonance. Therefore, you should consider smudging each drum in your home before beginning any serious shamanic work.

Selecting a drum

One of the most useful drums for shamanic work is the hand or frame drum. The frame drum originated in Siberia, together with shamanism itself. It has been associated worldwide with the practice of shamanism. The frame drum's resonance and versatility make it my drum of preference. Such drums are portable, affordable, and easy to play. They can easily be held in one hand, leaving the other hand free to stroke the drum. They are made by stretching a wet rawhide over a wooden frame, then allowing it to dry slowly. The frame or hoop is typically three inches or less in width and may vary from eight to twenty-four inches in diameter. They may be single-headed or double-headed. Like all rawhide drums, they do not have a fixed pitch. Heating and cooling the drumhead raises and lowers the tone.

Though I highly recommend frame drums, any type of drum may be used in shamanic drumming. There is a myriad of styles and drum types to choose from. Congas, doumbeks, djembes, ashikos, tablas, and timbales are but a few of the drum types readily available in music stores. In selecting a suitable drum, play several and listen for the drum that calls to you. You will know it by its voice. It will strike a deep chord within you.

Making a drum

Another possibility is to make your own drum. To guide you in drum making, I highly recommend the book, *How to Make Drums, Tomtoms, and Rattles: Primitive Percussion Instruments for Modern Use* by Bernard S. Mason. Crafting and playing a drum that you have made yourself is eminently more satisfying than playing any other. A drum of your own creation will be imbued with your own unique essence. It will become a powerful extension of your essential self. Moreover, the spirit of a drum will pass through your hands into the drum as you make it. As master drum maker Judith Thompson puts it, "Making a drum is like pulling your heart together and giving birth to a new part of yourself."[12]

The healing power of a drum is based on the trinity of spirits inherent in the animal skin and the tree that make up the drum and the human player who brings it to life. The spiritual essence of your drum will be determined by the materials that go into its construction. When choosing an animal skin for your drum, take into consideration what animal energies, abilities, and characteristics you would like to invoke. The skin is the vocal chord of the drum's spirit. Tuvan ethnographer Mongush Kenin-Lopsan explains, "Sounding the drum animates or enlivens it, giving voice to the spirit of the animal whose skin is struck with the beater."[13] Tuvan shamans often name their drums after the animals whose skins are stretched across their frames.

The birth of a shamanic drum adds a new branch to the World Tree/Tree of Life. The drum is connected to the World Tree through the wood of the frame and its association through all trees back to the First Tree. The cedar is known as the Tree of Life by various indigenous peoples; hence cedar wood is often used for drum frames. Cedar frame drums are both lightweight and resonant. Red and yellow cedar both work well.

In some cultures, the wood for the frame ideally comes from a lightning-struck tree, bringing the power of instantaneous transformation into the drum. Lightning here is also a metaphor for the striking clarity of the shaman's reborn soul as it rises from the ego death of his or her initiation.

Keep in mind that your drumstick or beater has a spirit and sound of its own. The best beaters for frame drums are made of strong hardwood with a padded, leather covered head. You can decorate your beater with fur, feathers, beadwork, or engrave sacred symbols into it. Different beaters work better with different drums to bring out the tone qualities. There are hard beaters, semi-hard beaters, soft beaters, and rattle beaters, which are simply beaters with a rawhide or gourd rattle attached to the base of the handle opposite the head. In Tuva, the rattle beater or *orba*, with its head covered with animal fur and metal rings attached for rattling, is in part for practicing divination and drawing the attention of the spirits. The snare sounds associated with metal, stone, and bone rattlers attached to beaters and drum frames are described as "spirit voices."

Waking the drum

When you make or acquire a new drum for shamanic work, it needs to be ritually awakened. This awakening process partly involves the mating of the unique resonance patterns of the drumhead and the frame. It is useful to smudge the drum and dedicate it to your work. Ask each of the seven powers or directions to bless your drum. Thank the animal spirit for giving its hide for your drum head. Thank the trees for your drum's wooden rim, and ask that the drum's hoop be connected to the World Tree, which enables all trees to sing your prayers while drumming.

Once you have invoked the spirits you normally work with, be sure to call upon the spirit of the drum and ask it to come to you and become your ally. Visualize yourself as a clean hollow bone, ready to be filled with hope, possibilities, and waiting to be filled with the spirit of your shamanic drum.

Now begin to gently play a heartbeat rhythm on your drum and, if you are doing this with other people, you set the tempo and rhythm of the drumming. Focus your attention on the sound of the drum, thereby opening yourself up to receive spirit. Allow the rhythm of the drum to become as natural as your breathing—a total expression of your being. Imagine the energy of your drum's spirit entering your hollow bone and traveling down into the earth. You may feel it, see it, sense it, or simply imagine it. Allow spirit to flow into and embody you so that your playing comes under its control. When embodying spirits, they will actually dictate the rhythm, tempo, volume, and timbre until you reach something that is suitable for them.

As the drum journey evolves, you will become more ecstatic and spirit will perhaps create new rhythms or cause you to sing. At some point in your journey, you will recognize that all of your helping spirits and power animals are traveling with you. They are at your side helping you become a living conduit for the spirit of the drum.

When it feels appropriate, gradually slow the tempo of your drumming to a regular heart beat rhythm to draw your consciousness back into your body. Do not rush the transformation. Visualize yourself fully grounded in your body, and then slowly open your eyes.

By embodying the spirit of your drum, a resonance occurs, like two sine waves overlapping in sync. As you resonate in sync with your drum, energy and awareness are exchanged. Communion with the drum's spirit is established.

When the spirit of the drum embodies you, it may teach you some special ways you can use the drum for your shamanic work that you did not know before. It may teach you a rhythm for invoking and enlivening it. When a helping spirit is invoked, there is often an accompanying rhythm that comes through. Be open to the possibilities.

Bonding with the spirit of a drum is a wondrous event. This kind of initiatory ceremony is a time of great celebration. When an awakening ritual is performed with many participants, the ceremony is followed by a festive meal in which the people rejoice that the spirits have brought the blessing of greater power to the keeper of the drum for the benefit of the community.

Care and feeding of your drum

In the shaman's world, all is alive. A drum is regarded as a living being: not as an object. As Tuvan shaman Lazo Mongush puts it, "A drum is a living organism. You have to feed it and take care of it."[14] The drum has a spirit that can be awakened and if called upon, must be fed. The spirits eat just as we eat. Shamans believe that if the spirits are not fed, the ritual may not go well. Shamans ritually feed their drums. Many use the head of the drum as an altar to offer blue cornmeal or tobacco to the spirit of the instrument. Cornmeal is good because corn is a sacred gift from the beings that live in the spirit world. The one offering the cornmeal first breathes on the grains so that the spirits know who is offering the gift. Offer the cornmeal to the four directions, and then to the drum itself so the spirit of the drum can eat it. You can offer a pinch of dry tobacco in the same manner. Tobacco, an herb with masculine and feminine medicine, feeds the drum and carries our prayers to the Loom of Creation, thereby reweaving the pattern of existence in accordance with those prayers.

Smudge smoke is also one of the foods for spirits. In Tuva, juniper smoke is offered to the spirit of the drum. Cedar, sage, and sweetgrass can also be used for the smudging and feeding of drums. To smudge your drum, light the herbs in a fire-resistant receptacle, and then blow out the flames. Smudge your drum by passing it through the smoke three times. Conclude the smudging by thanking the spirit of the plant or tree whose body made the cleansing possible.

Drums should be cared for in a manner befitting their place in your life. The most important thing to remember is that drums are alive and function best in the same conditions that humans find most comfortable. Basic care instructions are as follows:

1. Store your drum in a warm, dry place away from direct heat or sunshine. You can keep your drum in a water repellent nylon padded drum bag, or simply wrap it in a special cloth or animal hide.
2. Protect your drum from moisture. When your drum gets wet, the wood swells and the rawhide sags. You can clean your drum by rubbing it softly with a slightly damp cloth.
3. Never leave your drum in the car for any length of time in extreme heat or cold as this can split the head. Leaving your drum in direct sunlight for any length of time can also make the drum's head split.
4. When the humidity is high, you can restore the tone of your drum by heating it slowly with a hair dryer, in front of a fire, or on a heating pad. Avoid heating the skin to a temperature that is too hot to touch. You can preserve the tone of a drum by putting it in a tightly closed plastic bag.
5. In high-humidity areas, some people put some kind of a natural conditioner on their drumheads once a year. You can rub a light coating of lanolin or neatsfoot oil into the back of the drumhead and on the cords. Your drum will stay in tune longer and absorb less moisture.
6. If a painted design on your drumhead is starting to wear away, you can touch it up with acrylic paint. After your paint has dried, apply a coat of clear acrylic sealer to the entire drumhead using a wide brush or spray the design with clear matte art fixative.
7. Should your drum ever require repair, consult the person who crafted the drum. If that is not possible, find another drum maker who works in a similar way. If you can find someone to teach you how to repair the drum, it's well worth the time to do so.

With minimal care, your drum will last for many years as a trusted ally. The very first drum I made is over twenty years old and shows no signs of deterioration despite extensive use. The simplest way to care for your drum is to play it. A drum is not meant to be left hanging on a wall as a decoration. It is a sacred instrument that opens portals to the spirit world. Each time you pick up your drum, thank it, honor it, and express your gratitude for this gift from a greater being.

Also consider releasing the word "mine" when it comes to the drum you carry. As a drum keeper, you are the caretaker of the drum's spirit: you cannot own it. "Release your drum's spirit from the very start of your journey so that it may free your spirit later!"[15]

Journey drumming recordings

A recent development in shamanic journeywork is the use of compact disc recordings of shamanic drumming. When used with a high quality stereo with optimal bass response, a sympathetic resonance between the drums and the body-consciousness is provided. The effects are similar to those of having a real drum in the room. The healing vibrations of a recording may lack the intensity of the actual drum, yet it allows complete freedom to journey without the necessity of placing part of the conscious mind on the physical aspects of playing a drum. It takes time and practice to relax and allow the intuitive mind to flow, while at the same time maintaining an even rhythmic pattern. Portable compact disc players with headphones allow you to alter your consciousness anywhere and anytime without disturbing others or when using a drum may be impractical. However, one should avoid listening to such recordings while driving a vehicle or operating heavy machinery. There are times when entering trance states is inappropriate, so use discretion.

I recently released the CD *Shamanic Journey Drumming* to support the listener in making shamanic journeys.[16] The overtone harmonics on this recording were produced by a twenty-two-inch single-headed, elk skin, red cedar frame drum pulsed at four beats per second. When pulsed at four beats per second, rhythmic drumming induces a theta wave cycle in the brain. Theta activity reflects the dreamlike state between wakefulness and sleep. Theta rhythms are associated with meditation, prayer, spiritual awareness, and the deepest states of shamanic consciousness. Theta increases creativity, enhances learning, reduces stress, and awakens intuition.

Journey drumming recordings provide a relatively easy means of controlled transcendence. Researchers have found that if a drum beat frequency of around four beats per second is sustained for at least fifteen minutes, most novices report that they can journey successfully even on their first attempt.[17] Shamanic drumming continues to offer today what it has offered for thousands of years: namely, a simple and effective technique of ecstasy.

Chapter 9

Shamanic Drumming Circles

Drumming creates in the psyche of those people who listen to the drum, a sense of abundance, a feeling that there is more than enough in life to sustain life. There is the feeling of strength, of being able to step forth with whatever one wants to change because the power to sustain that change is in the drumming.
—Joseph Rael, *Being and Vibration* [1]

Everyone experiences moments that forever change them. On April 28, 2007, I enjoyed an entire day of peak experiences. It was one of those magical days that you never forget. I was very present in the moment nearly every moment of the day. It was the Saturday before the celestially auspicious May Day or Beltane, and I was facilitating an experiential workshop on shamanic drumming at the Central Oregon Environmental Center in Bend, Oregon. We had gathered a circle of thirty drummers with four large ceremonial community drums sitting in the four directions. We opened the circle with the sounding of four conch trumpets, each pointed at one of the four cardinal directions.

I then called in the spirits, shaking a beautiful Mexican rain stick in the form of Quetzalcoatl, the Feathered Serpent, carved in dark wood. Many indigenous cultures believe the sound of gently falling rain produced by rain sticks creates a storm. As I invoked the powers of the seven directions, I called in the Thunder Beings: thunder, lightning, wind, and rain. I asked the Thunder Beings to bestow their enlightenment upon us as the lightning enlightens the earth. Through lightning they directly purify the air we breathe, the water we drink, and the earth we cultivate. The Thunder Beings are the force behind all weather changes and sustain life on earth. They travel in the clouds and lightning and speak through the thunder. Their medicine and gift is balance, change, and renewal.

The Thunder Beings are a force for both dissolution and re-creation. They are nature's way of breaking down the archetypal patterns of an old cycle in preparation for a new cycle. Divergent polar forces pull apart obsolete patterns, allowing new patterns to form. According to Taoist Thunder-specialist Samudranath, through the Thunder Beings, "all life has been initiated or created, is sustained, and will be destroyed. In all traditions it is Thunder-beings who govern nature and all life; they are the Creators. They sustain balanced life, and destroy imbalance, the cause of suffering."[2]

The Thunder Beings proclaim the sacred union of Father Sky and Mother Earth through bolts of lightning. Like thunderbolts, we humans are a bridge that connects earth and sky. Like Mother Earth and Father Sky, we are both yin/female and yang/male in nature. Only when yin and yang are in balance within us, are we able to effectively channel usable energy. Achieving balance requires that we release our fears, plow old habits under, and cultivate new growth. By asking the Thunderers to assist us in achieving balance, we learn how to tap into their energy and utilize it creatively. We learn how to revitalize ourselves and grow.

In the Plains shamanic traditions, a person who is visited by a Thunder Being in a dream, a vision, or in person becomes a heyoka or "contrary." Customarily, this heyoka then begins to behave in ways that are contrary to the conventional norms of the dominant culture. The heyoka behaves in such a manner in order to awaken society to innovative and better ways of doing things. Thus, the heyoka becomes the human counterpart of the Thunder Beings, who continually break down the existing order and create a new arrangement from the pieces.

The negative power of the present World cannot be obliterated. It can only be transmuted by being confronted by the contrary behavior of the heyokas—the paradoxical energy of thunder and lightning. Like the crash of thunder, violating peoples' expectations can startle and awaken them. In such paradoxical states, people can assimilate new information quickly, without filtering. We are not alone in this task. The Thunder Beings have come to awaken us, to test us, and to help us transmute the world's negative energies into peaceful, balanced, and harmonious energies.

Because there is such great turmoil in the world today, it would be beneficial if more of us established an intimate relationship with the Thunder Beings. We can relate to them in storms and nature, but primarily we must seek them within. The drum can help us immeasurably in this quest. The drum embodies the creative spirit and energy of the Thunder Beings. The drum, like the Thunder Beings, is a catalyst that unites masculine and feminine energies, generating life force. It quickens us with the vital energy needed to confront the world's dissonant negative energies and transmute them into peaceful, balanced, and harmonious energies. The drum is a safe and powerful vehicle for traversing the inner world, which is a microcosm of the outer world.

After calling the spirits, I held a prayer feather in my right hand and spoke a prayer for our relative the honey bee, who is rapidly disappearing worldwide due to a phenomenon known as colony collapse disorder. Colony collapse is significant because many flowering plants, trees, and agricultural crops worldwide are pollinated by bees. I then passed the feather around the circle so that each participant could hold it and put their prayers and intention into the feather. After the prayer feather circled the room, I placed it on the altar in the center of the circle.

After offering prayers, we drummed the four archetypal rhythms of the Thunder Beings—thunder, lightning, wind, and rain—to create a storm to overcome static tensions, clearing the way for the rainbow of peace and harmony (see my CD *Thunder Beings Journey Drumming*).[3] The greater the obstructions to harmony, the more destructive the storm must be in order to clear away those obstructions. Storm represents that moment when the clouds gather, lightning strikes, and the rain bursts forth—a quintessentially creative moment.

As each round of the "thunder drumming" progressed, I felt myself undergoing complete dismemberment and being scattered by the winds to the four directions and then being reformed or reborn. I experienced this repeatedly: being blown apart and then recreated. I saw jagged bolts of lightning rip through me and others in the circle. I then sensed a peaceful ebb and flow like the universe breathing in and out. I felt centered, balanced, and empowered.

When we joined our hands together to close the drum circle, the current flowing through the palms of my hands was electric. The flow was so strong that I could barely hold my grip. We thanked the spirits for their blessings and presence, and then sent them off to wherever they needed to be.

After the closing ceremony, we stepped outside and were met by a large colony of honey bees swarming in the street in front of the environmental center. The buzzing vortex of honey bees was as wide as the street and around twenty feet tall. We stood in stunned silence for about ten minutes, watching the spectacle unfold. From the chaos came order and organization. The colony eventually clustered around the queen in a shrub in the front yard of the environmental center.

I found the synchronicity between my prayer for the honey bee and the manifestation of an entire bee colony to be quite extraordinary. I later learned that, earlier that morning, the city of Bend had taken upon itself to evict the bee colony from its nest in Drake Park in downtown Bend. Apparently, the bees posed a potential threat to park users. The refugee bee colony swarmed about eight city blocks from Drake Park to begin anew at the sanctuary of the Central Oregon Environmental Center.

During the afternoon of the following day, a severe thunderstorm rumbled through Central Oregon, bringing heavy rain and up to six inches of hail. The storm spawned flash floods, damaging winds, and thousands of lightning strikes. The electricity of lightning touching down purified the domain of all beings, destroying harmful influences, such as diseases that choke off life. The vernal storm made the earth pliant and fresh, suitable for spontaneous growth and balanced transformation. Through the lightning, all life is created, sustained, and eventually destroyed.

The healing power of the drum circle

Indigenous cultures have been practicing community percussion for thousands of years. Although most of us did not grow up in an indigenous rhythmic musical tradition, we can still tap into the healing power of the root rhythmic patterns that underlie our resonant field of reality. The nature of culture creation is that traditions take root whenever a group of people makes a commitment to do things together in a particular way and sustains that commitment over time. I am grateful to be part of a community that has drummed and journeyed together for nearly twenty years. When we come together in rhythm, not just once in a while, but repeatedly and consistently, we co-create a container in which the archetypes of rhythm evolve into a force for healing our community.

The shamanic drumming circle is the most powerful way I know to connect with the spirit and oneness of everything. Drum circles provide the opportunity for people of like mind to unite for the attainment of a shared objective. There is power in drumming alone, but that power recombines and multiplies on many simultaneous levels in a group of drummers. The drums draw individual energies together, unifying them into a consolidated force that can be channeled toward the circle's intended goal.

Shamanic drumming should be done in unison so that the drumming creates a mesmerizing effect to induce trance. Avoid free form drumming, which produces a cacophony of competing beats. The goal is to produce a sound that is unifying and consciousness-shifting, so individuals should alternate the responsibility of setting the tempo and leading the drum circle. Like the indigenous shaman who conducts community healing rites, the drum circle facilitator must guide the pattern, flow, and energy of the drumming toward the ritual's intended goal. The basic steps that I find most effective are as follows:

1. Simply join together, forming a circle. By creating a circle, you are structuring an energy pattern that will contain, focus, and amplify the power generated by drumming. Like the hoop of the drum, the circle represents the wheel of life and shared community. All are equal in the circle; no one is above or below. In a circle, each person's face can be seen; each person's voice can be heard and valued. Together the drummers create the necessary rhythmic container that channels the outpouring of energy toward the intended objective.

2. Next, you should purify and open your sacred space. Be creative in this process. Blowing a conch trumpet will clear out unwanted energies and announce to the spirits that ceremony is beginning. Bells, gongs, and Tibetan singing bowls help purify and enliven sacred space. Remember that the flute, drum, and rattle represent the whole voice of Creation.

3. Before smudging inside a gathering place, be aware that some participants may have severe respiratory diseases, and that smoldering smudge may set off a smoke alarm, so take appropriate precautions. Consider smudging participants outside the building or dwelling if smudging inside is unfeasible. To smudge the space and all participants, pass a smudge bowl clockwise around the circle. Each person can then smudge themselves and their drum. Remember that smudge offerings, prayer feathers, or power objects are customarily accepted with the left hand and then passed on to the next person in the circle with the right hand.

131

4. At this point, you should invoke the powers of the seven directions. The facilitator can lead the group in this process. I like to have the participants stand and face each direction in unison. Use your right hand, or hold a feather in your right hand to fan smudge offerings to the East. If you have a rattle, shake it four times to open a portal in the East to the spirit world. Using words, chanting, or song, invite the helping spirits associated with that direction to participate and assist in the ceremony. Pivot around clockwise and repeat the same procedure to summon the spirits of the South, the West, the North, Father Sky above, Mother Earth below, and finally face the center of the circle to invite the spirit of Within. Call upon the spirit of divine unity that flows from within the center of your being where the six directions meet.

5. Having invoked the seven directions, it is important to form the group's collective intention or goal. After clarifying the intended objective, I like to pass a prayer feather around the circle so that each participant can hold it and put their prayers and intention into the feather. After the prayer feather circles the room, I place it on an altar in the center of the circle. You can also place photos of loved ones on the altar so that they are included in your prayers to the spirits. Remember that your altar is the center and axis of your sacred space.

6. The next step is to begin the prayer round of drumming. A steady eagle-beat pulsed at three to four beats per second is the most effective. This rhythm will carry the group's intention and awareness into the heavenly realm of archetypes that shape and direct our reality. All participants should now focus their attention on the group intention to seed the blueprint of the desired outcome. As they focus on it, it will occur, for energy and life force follow thought. It is the responsibility of the facilitator to guide the group in this process. When leading a group, I move the beater around the drumhead until I find the sweet spot and my drum begins to sing and hum. Eventually, I can hear the sound of my drum moving around the circle, resonating through each person's drum. The drums begin to sing in unison, and I sense that each person is connected to the Celestial Realm. I try to hold this energy dynamic for as long as possible. This climactic phase eventually wanes, and the drums start doing their own thing again. This is usually the point where I signal the end of the first round of drumming with four thundering beats of the drum.

7. Once the group intention has been introduced, begin the healing round of drumming. Stroke a slow, steady heartbeat rhythm; gradually building up the intensity to a tempo of about three to four beats per second. This healing pulse is magnetic and receptive in nature, drawing awareness, archetypal knowledge, and transpersonal powers down into the material world. It gives form and substance to the pattern of the group intention. The heartbeat also draws the energy of the original cosmological pattern down into the earthly realm, helping to align the drum circle and the circle of life with the original intention for the earth. Participants should now clear their minds of everything. We must surrender all attachment to the desired outcome to achieve success. It is best to close our eyes and focus on the sound of the drum. Allow the spirit of the drum to do the healing. The drum spirits will generate, access, and direct life force energy based solely on our original intention.

8. When you feel the power ebbing, signal the end of the second round of drumming with four booming beats.

9. Commence the thank you round of drumming with the even cadence of the eagle-beat. Sustain a tempo of three to four beats per second for one to five minutes. Participants should give thanks for the needs met and the needs they are asking to be met.

10. Finally, signal the end of the drumming with four resounding beats. It is important to conclude the drumming circle by closing sacred space. I like to begin this process by having everyone stand and join hands in a circle for closing prayers. Each person should have an opportunity to speak if they choose. To ritually close sacred space, follow the same procedure as for the opening, but in reverse order. Begin by thanking the spiritual energies of Within, Mother Earth and Father Sky, and then the North, the West, the South and the East in a counterclockwise movement. This counterclockwise movement will close the energy vortex and signal that the sacred time of focus is ended. Express your gratitude to the archetypal elements and helping spirits for being with you and send them off, releasing their energies to the seven directions. The drum circle is followed by a festive meal in which the people rejoice that the spirits have brought the blessing of greater power to the community.

Shamanic drumming circles are an effective way to heal and harmonize the web of life. The drums shape available energy into a powerful vortex that spirals out into the resonating circle of life. Drum circles open portals to the spirit world and facilitate a merging of the physical and spiritual realms. They expedite communication with helping spirits and draw them in. The drumming circle also links the consciousness of each participant to the vibrant life force of the oneness of all things. It develops a continuous, shared consciousness with all our relations. Even small groups of people of one mind, one purpose, and fully attuned through the drums can transform the world and manifest what is needed to benefit all beings.

The therapeutic effects of drumming circles

Current research is now verifying the therapeutic effects of drumming circles. Recent research reviews indicate that group drumming accelerates physical healing, boosts the immune system and produces feelings of well-being, a release of emotional trauma, and reintegration of self. Other studies have demonstrated the calming, focusing, and healing effects of drumming on Alzheimer's patients, autistic children, emotionally disturbed teens, recovering addicts, trauma patients, and prison and homeless populations. Study results demonstrate that drumming is a valuable treatment for stress, fatigue, anxiety, hypertension, asthma, chronic pain, arthritis, mental illness, migraines, cancer, multiple sclerosis, Parkinson's disease, stroke, paralysis, emotional disorders, and a wide range of physical disabilities. Research studies mentioned below indicate that group drumming:

Reduces tension, anxiety, and stress

Drumming induces deep relaxation, lowers blood pressure, and reduces stress. Stress, according to current medical research, contributes to nearly all disease and is a primary cause of such life-threatening illnesses as heart attacks, strokes, and immune system breakdowns. A recent study found that a program of group drumming helped reduce stress and employee turnover in the long-term care industry and might help other high-stress occupations as well.[4]

Helps control chronic pain

Chronic pain has a progressively draining effect on the quality of life. Researchers suggest that drumming serves as a distraction from pain and grief. Moreover, drumming promotes the production of endorphins and endogenous opiates, the bodies own morphine-like painkillers, and can thereby help in the control of pain.[5]

Boosts the immune system

A recent medical research study indicates that group drumming reverses the classic stress response, which depresses immune system function. Led by renowned cancer expert Barry Bittman, MD, the study demonstrates that community drumming actually increases natural killer cell activity, one of the mechanisms through which the body combats cancer and viral illnesses, including AIDS. According to Dr. Bittman, "Group drumming tunes our biology, orchestrates our immunity, and enables healing to begin."[6]

Accesses the entire brain

The reason rhythm is such a powerful tool is that it permeates the entire brain. Vision for example is in one part of the brain, speech another, but drumming accesses the whole brain. The sound of drumming generates dynamic neuronal connections in all parts of the brain even where there is significant damage or impairment such as in Attention Deficit Disorder (ADD). According to Michael Thaut, director of Colorado State University's Center for Biomedical Research in Music, "Rhythmic cues can help retrain the brain after a stroke or other neurological impairment, as with Parkinson's patients ...." The more connections that can be made within the brain, the more integrated our experiences become.

Induces natural altered states of consciousness

Rhythmic drumming induces altered states, which have a wide range of therapeutic applications. A recent study by Barry Quinn, Ph.D. demonstrates that even a brief drumming session can double alpha brain wave activity, dramatically reducing stress.[7] The brain changes from Beta waves (focused concentration and activity) to Alpha waves (calm and relaxed), producing feelings of euphoria and well-being. Alpha activity is associated with meditation, shamanic trance, and integrative modes of consciousness. This ease of induction contrasts significantly with the long periods of isolation and practice required by most meditative disciplines before inducing significant effects. Rhythmic stimulation is a simple yet effective technique for affecting states of mind.

Creates a sense of connectedness with self and others

In a society in which traditional family and community-based systems of support have become increasingly fragmented, drumming circles provide a sense of connectedness with others and interpersonal support. A drumming circle provides an opportunity to connect with your own spirit at a deeper level, and also to connect with a group of other like-minded people. Group drumming alleviates self-centeredness, isolation, and alienation. Music educator Ed Mikenas finds that drumming provides "an authentic experience of unity and physiological synchronicity. If we put people together who are out of sync with themselves (i.e., diseased, addicted) and help them experience the phenomenon of entrainment, it is possible for them to feel with and through others what it is like to be synchronous in a state of preverbal connectedness."[8]

Releases negative feelings, blockages, and emotional trauma

Drumming can help people express and address emotional issues. Unexpressed feelings and emotions can form energy blockages. The physical stimulation of drumming removes blockages and produces emotional release. Sound vibrations resonate through every cell in the body, stimulating the release of negative cellular memories. "Drumming emphasizes self-expression, teaches how to rebuild emotional health, and addresses issues of violence and conflict through expression and integration of emotions," says music educator Ed Mikenas. Drumming can also address the needs of addicted populations by helping them learn to deal with their emotions in a therapeutic way without the use of drugs. In his 2003 article, "Drumming Out Drugs," Michael Winkelman reports, "Drumming circles and other shamanic altered states of consciousness activities can address multiple needs of addicted populations."[9]

Places one in the present moment

Drumming helps alleviate stress that is created from hanging on to the past or worrying about the future. When one plays a drum, one is placed squarely in the here and now. One of the paradoxes of rhythm is that it has both the capacity to move your awareness out of your body into realms beyond time and space and to ground you firmly in the present moment. It allows you to maintain a portion of ordinary awareness while experiencing non-ordinary awareness. This permits full recall later of the visionary experience.

Provides a medium for individual self-realization

Drumming provides a means of exploring and developing the inner self. In his book, *Being and Vibration*, Ute-Tiwa shaman Joseph Rael explains, "Drumming opens up three basic vibrations. Drumming awakens the self. Drumming heightens the ability of perception, and drumming enables the person to see into the deeper realms of the self."[10] Drumming reconnects us to our core, enhancing our sense of empowerment and stimulating our creative expression.

According to music educator Edward Mikenas, "The advantage of participating in a drumming group is that you develop an auditory feedback loop within yourself and among group members—a channel for self-expression and positive feedback—that is pre-verbal, emotion-based, and sound-mediated."[11] Each person in a drum circle is expressing themselves through his or her drum and listening to the other drums at the same time. "Everyone is speaking, everyone is heard, and each person's sound is an essential part of the whole."[12] Each person can drum out their feelings without saying a word, without having to reveal their issues. Group drumming complements traditional talk therapy methods. The primitive drumming circle is emerging as a significant therapeutic tool in the modern technological age.

Afterword

In October 2011, I felt spirit calling me. Mother Earth is birthing a new beginning. She is dissolving the existing order and fashioning a new arrangement from the pieces. The earthquakes, erupting volcanoes, tsunamis and climate changes are the birth pangs of this new world. As her birth pangs grew stronger and stronger, I felt compelled to travel to the sacred sites that beckoned me. I followed my deepest instincts. I traveled with my drum, medicine bundle, and helping spirits to shamanize the meridian system of her numinous web, which is the planetary counterpart to the acupuncture meridian system of the human body.

Early man discovered these planetary currents called ley lines. In China, they were known as dragon currents. The Aborigines of Australia know them as a line of songs. In England, the Druids referred to the old straight track. Native Americans regarded the energy channels as the serpent power or the great dragons. According to Cherokee mythology, the dragons once followed the will of the great shamans who would invoke them to protect the people and the land.

These energy ley lines contain a two-fold element, a male and female, positive and negative, expanding and reverting breath, resembling two magnetic currents—the azure dragon and the white tiger. At the intersection points of the planet's energy web exist holy places, power spots, or acupuncture points. Like acupuncture needles, humans are capable of maintaining the harmonious flow of the planetary energy meridians by making an earth connection at power places.

Many magical things happened during my two month pilgrimage. I soaked in the healing waters of Umpqua, Buckeye, Travertine, Whitmore, and Keough Hot Springs. I camped at Panther Meadows on Mount Shasta. I hiked among the oldest living things on the earth in the Ancient Bristlecone Pine Forest.

By happenstance, I encountered my dear friend and master drum maker Judith Thomson in Bishop, California. Judith and I began facilitating workshops together in 1993. She was called by spirit to teach drum making and I was called to teach shamanic drumming. Unbeknownst to me,

Judith had journeyed from her home in Packwood, Washington to facilitate a drum making seminar in Big Pine, California. I helped Judith teach her final class before retirement, and she helped me and thirteen other participants birth the most beautiful singing drums I have ever heard.

After the seminar, Judith returned to Packwood, and I was asked to stay for a drum blessing and workshop the following weekend after the wet rawhide drums had dried. The drum awakening ceremony was held outside next to Birch Creek. We asked each of the seven powers/directions to bless our drums. We thanked the animal spirits for giving their skins for our drum heads. We thanked the trees for the wooden rims and asked that the hoops of our drums be connected to the World Tree, which enables all trees to sing our prayers while drumming. Our drums were consecrated and we journeyed to meet our power animals.

The azure dragon

Over the next six weeks, I facilitated two more workshops, taught classes, and administered drum therapy treatments in a creek-side yurt at the base of Birch Mountain on the east side of the Sierra Nevada crest. It is here that a guardian dragon began to appear in my dreams, meditations, and shamanic journeys. The Sierra Nevada range embodies the spirit of a great green dragon. The azure mountain dragon has empowered my life immeasurably. Dragon carries me higher and deeper into myself than any energy I know.

Dragon medicine represents wisdom, protection, magic, transformation, shapeshifting, and the inner knowing of the true self. Dragon's power is that of shedding its skin and coming out as a new, transformed being. Dragon transmutes with the mastery of the infinite self, bringing us to the culmination of our multi-dimensional existence. Dragon is among our strongest allies on the path of self-realization and offers us fierce protection.

According to Cherokee wisdom keeper Dhyani Ywahoo, the energy of the *Ukdena*, or great dragons, used to protect this land, but the dragons have now become tied into the mountains or moved into another dimension. She believes that the connection between these dragons and the mind of humans is significant in these changing times. Ywahoo explains, "Basically, the dragon is the unconscious of all nations, the untamed energies of anger and fear, waiting to be called into the light of clear thought. Until people awaken to their own minds, the dragon appears to be dangerous; when emotions are tamed, the dragon becomes a winged angelic being."[1]

The white tiger

Prior to my final workshop at Mammoth Lakes on December 7th, I planned a four day desert exploration. In one day I drove from Mt. Whitney (the sacred masculine), the tallest mountain in the continuous 48 states, into Death Valley (the sacred feminine), the lowest elevation in North America. Shortly after entering Death Valley National Park, I took an eight mile detour north along the Saline Valley Road to visit a Joshua Tree forest at Lee Flat. The Saline Valley Road is very rough and progress was slow, but I eventually reached the magical forest. A cold wind buffeted me each time I left the confines of my truck to hike and photograph the forest. I would have camped here for the night if not for the high elevation and bitter cold wind (winds follow the tiger). I camped instead at Panamint Springs Resort, 22 miles inside the western border of Death Valley National Park.

The following day, I explored Darwin Falls and the remote Panamint Valley adjacent to Death Valley. I camped for the next few days at the far northeast end of the South Panamint Dry Lake, a small wetland, grassland, dune system and mesquite bosque. The warm sulphur springs of this desert oasis provide habitat for frogs, shore birds, marsh hawks, and wild burros. A short-eared owl visited my campsite each evening at dusk and a white tiger prowled my dreams each night. The stars bathed the cold desert in a warm glow. Few things are more serene than the deep stillness of the desert on a starry night. In that stillness, I am reborn, forever changed.

Oh, how I love vagabonding. Shamanism is deeply rooted in nature and a nomadic lifestyle. The emphasis is on the individual, of breaking free and discovering one's own uniqueness in order to bring something new back to the group. Like drumming, nomadic wandering alters your ordinary everyday awareness. It is another means of habitual pattern disruption for reimprinting on alternate realties. When you leave home, meet new people, experience new stimuli, and process new information, you're soon intoxicated on a natural high. As Ed Buryn, the godfather of modern vagabonding puts it, "Vagabonding is nothing less than reality transformation, and its power is not to be underestimated."[2]

A pilgrimage is a journey of self-discovery. It is essentially meeting people, and every person that I meet enriches my life in some remarkable way, even if I don't realize it at the time. The people we meet do not appear by chance. Though the spirits are the best teachers, they are not the only ones, for life's journey puts many people on the same path, people from whom we can learn. The journey continues; the learning continues.

Becoming a shamanic practitioner

In his monumental work, *Shamanism: Archaic Techniques of Ecstasy*, Mircea Eliade describes the three stages of becoming a shaman: the Call, Training, and Initiation. In their book, *Shaman Wisdom, Shaman Healing*, Michael Samuels and Mary Rockwood Lane have taken Eliade's three stages and added a fourth: "the practice of shamanism."[3] To be an effective shaman, one must go through the three stages of development, and ultimately the practice of shamanism in the community. An authentic shamanic practitioner makes a commitment to intercede between the spiritual and human realms on behalf of the local community. It's an alliance that fosters healing, problem solving, and strong communities.

Shamanism is a sacred call to build relationship. A skillful shamanic practitioner works in sacred partnership with helping spirits—the power animals, the benevolent ancestors, and the sacred elements. Spirit helpers are the caretakers in the unseen world who want to support the earth and her inhabitants at this time. They are here to teach us how to gather wisdom from the spiritual realms, the natural world, the past, the present, and the future in order to give birth to new ways of being.

The shamanic relationship between humans and helping spirits supports our spirit's quest for self-realization. Helping spirits, if engaged regularly and skillfully, offer flexibility, creativity, and perseverance in fulfilling our own unique path. The spirits are here to teach us to be better humans. They come to assist us in doing the principal unique thing we have come here to do in a way that benefits all living things.

Shamanism offers a valid and effective path back to our soul and its purpose for being here. By engaging life from a shamanic perspective, we rediscover our core values and deep loves, find others who share them, and recommit our lives to living from what has heart and meaning. The passionate expression of our soul's purpose is precisely the medicine the earth needs at this time.

We can engage the blueprint of our soul path through the vehicle of drumming. Shamanic drumming is a time-tested medium for individual self-realization. It provides a means of exploring and developing the inner self. We can journey within to access wisdom and energies that can help awaken our soul calling and restore us to wholeness. Drumming reconnects us with our deepest core values and our highest vision of who we are and why we are here. It heightens our sense of mission and purpose, empowering our personal evolution.

Integrating shamanic experience

Recent studies have demonstrated that shamanic drumming produces deeper self-awareness by inducing synchronous brain activity. The physical transmission of rhythmic energy to the brain synchronizes the two cerebral hemispheres, integrating conscious and unconscious awareness. The ability to access unconscious information through symbols and imagery facilitates psychological integration and a reintegration of self.

In his book, *Shamanism: The Neural Ecology of Consciousness and Healing*, Michael Winkelman reports that drumming also synchronizes the frontal and lower areas of the brain, integrating nonverbal information from lower brain structures into the frontal cortex, producing "feelings of insight, understanding, integration, certainty, conviction, and truth, which surpass ordinary understandings and tend to persist long after the experience, often providing foundational insights for religious and cultural traditions."[4]

It requires abstract thinking and the interconnection between symbols, concepts, and emotions to process unconscious information. The human adaptation to translate an inner trance experience into meaningful narrative is uniquely exploited by singing, vocalizing, and drumming. Shamanic music targets memory, perception, and the complex emotions associated with symbols and concepts: the principal functions humans rely on to formulate belief. Because of this exploit, the result of the synchronous brain activity in humans is the spontaneous generation of meaningful information which is imprinted into memory.

Shamanic experience can be expressed in many ways: through writing, art, and film, however, it must be created after the fact. The one artistic medium which can be used to immediately express shamanic trance without disrupting the quality of the experience is music. The shaman's use of sound and rhythm is an audible reflection of their inner environment. This is the traditional method for integrating shamanic experience into both physical space and the cultural group.

Endnotes

Introduction

1. Michael Winkelman, *Shamanism: A Biopsychosocial Paradigm of Consciousness and Healing* (Praeger; 2 edition 2010), p. 38.
2. Michael Winkelman. *Shamanism as Neurotheology and Evolutionary Psychology.* Tech. 13 May 2002. Web. 28 Feb. 2012. <http://www.public.asu.edu/~atmxw/absneuro.pdf>.
3. Michael Winkelman, "Complementary Therapy for Addiction: Drumming Out Drugs," *American Journal of Public Health*; Apr 2003, Vol. 93 Issue 4, p647, 5p.
4. Christina Pratt, *An Encyclopedia of Shamanism* (The Rosen Publishing Group, 2007), p. xxii.
5. Kenneth Cohen, *Honoring the Medicine: The Essential Guide to Native American Healing* (Random House Publishing Group, 2006), p. 217.
6. Wynne Hanner. "Awakening into Dreamtime: The Shaman's Journey." *Planet Shifter Magazine.* 3 Aug. 2011. Web. 2 Mar. 2012. <http://www.planetshifter.com/node/1912>.
7. Christina Pratt, *An Encyclopedia of Shamanism* (The Rosen Publishing Group, 2007), p. 151.
8. Kira Van Deusen, *Singing Story, Healing Drum: Shamans and Storytellers of Turkic Siberia* (McGill-Queen's Press, 2005), p. 122.
9. Kira Van Deusen, "Shamanism and Music in Tuva and Khakassia," *Shaman's Drum*, No. 47, Winter 1997, p. 26.
10. John Neihardt, *Black Elk Speaks: Being the Life Story of a Holy Man of the Oglala Sioux* (New York: Simon & Schuster, 1959), p. 71.
11. Felicitas D. Goodman, *Jewels on the Path: A Spirit Notebook*, vol. II (Santa Fe: Cuyamungue Institute, 1994), p. 55.
12. John Neihardt, *Black Elk Speaks*, p. 71.
13. Van Deusen, "Shamanism and Music in Tuva and Khakassia," p. 24.
14. Ted Andrews, *Animal Speak: The Spiritual & Magical Powers of Creatures Great & Small* (Llewellyn Publications, 1996), p. 93.
15. Sarangerel Odigon, *Chosen by the Spirits: Following Your Shamanic Calling* (Destiny Books, 2001), p. 9.

Chapter 1: The Calling

1. George Leonard, *The Silent Pulse*, (New York: Bantam New Age Books, 1981).
2. Edward Abbey, *Desert Solitaire: A Season in the Wilderness* (Touchstone, 1990), p. 167.

Chapter 2: The Initiation

1. Sandra Ingerman. "Messages from Sandra Ingerman." *Transmutation News* (Mar. 2011): 1.*Sandra Ingerman*. 1 Mar. 2011. Web. 6 Feb. 2012. <http://www.sandraingerman.com/tnmarch2011.html>.
2. Richard Whiteley. "Global Dismemberment: Through the Shaman's Eye." Interview. *Why Shamanism Now*. 21 Sept. 2011. Web. 3 Feb. 2012. <http://whyshamanismnow.com/2011/09/global-dismemberment-through-the-shaman%E2%80%99s-eye-with-richard-whiteley/>.
3. Felicitas D. Goodman, *Where the Spirits Ride the Wind: Trance Journeys and Other Ecstatic Experiences* (Indiana University Press,1990).
4. Joan Halifax, *Shamanic Voices: A Survey of Visionary Narratives* (Penguin, 1991), p. 18.
5. Halifax, *Shamanic Voices*, p. 22.
6. Daniel Pinchbeck, *2012: The Return of Quetzalcoatl* (Tarcher, 2006), p. 72.

Chapter 3: The Training

1. Terrence McKenna. "Shamanism." Lecture. Matrix Masters. Web. 28 Feb. 2012. <http://www.matrixmasters.net/podcasts/TRANSCRIPTS/TMcK-Shamanism1.html>.
2. Henry David Thoreau, *Walden and Other Writings* (Modern Library, 1950), p. 81.
3. Byron Harvey III, "An Overview of Pueblo Religion." *New Perspectives on the Pueblos*, Ed. Alfonso Ortiz (Albuquerque: University of New Mexico, 1980), p. 206.
4. Jade Wah'oo Grigori. "Grandfather Fire and the Circle of Animal Brothers." Lecture. Shamanic Drumming Circle. Sedona. 27 Mar. 1989. Shamanic. 22 July 2009. Web. 9 Feb. 2012. <http://www.shamanic.net/index.php/articles/67-article-circle-of-animal-brothers>.
5. Jade Wah'oo Grigori. "Shamanic Drumming." Lecture. Shamanic Drumming Circle. Sedona. 27 Mar. 1989. Shamanic. 12 July 2009. Web. 9 Feb. 2012. <http://www.shamanic.net/index.php/articles/40-shamanicdrumming>.
6. Sule Greg Wilson, *The Drummer's Path* (Rochester: Destiny Books, 1992), p. 76.
7. Richard Wilhelm. *The I Ching* (Princeton: Princeton University Press, 1967), p 238.
8. Terrence McKenna. "Shamanism." Lecture. Matrix Masters. Web. 28 Feb. 2012. <http://www.matrixmasters.net/podcasts/TRANSCRIPTS/TMcK-Shamanism1.html>.
9. Michael Drake, *The Shamanic Drum: A Guide to Sacred Drumming* (Talking Drum Publications, 1991).

Chapter 4: Helping Spirits

1. Christina Pratt, "Spirit Teachers and Better Humans." *Why Shamanism Now*. 12 Apr. 2011.*Why Shamanism Now*. 13 Apr. 2011. Web. 28 Feb. 2012. <http://whyshamanismnow.com/2011/04/spirit-teachers-and-better-humans/>.
2. Chief John Snow, *These Mountains Are Our Sacred Places* (Toronto: Samuel Stevens, 1977), p. 3.

3. Michael Harner, *The Way of the Shaman: A Guide to Power and Healing* (New York: Bantam edition, 1982), p 104.

Chapter 5: Creating Sacred Space

1. Christiana Harle-Silvennoinen, "In the Land of Song and the Drum: Receiving Inspiration from Tuvan Shamans," *Sacred Hoop*, Issue 25, 1999.
2. Wallace Black Elk and William S. Lyon, *Black Elk: The Sacred Ways of a Lakota* (San Francisco: Harper & Row, 1990), p. 149.
3. Joseph Rael and Mary Marlow, *Being and Vibration* (Tulsa: Council Oak Books, 1993), p 185.
4. Kenneth Johnson, *Jaguar Wisdom: Mayan Calendar Magic* (Llewellyn Pub.; 1997), p. 20.

Chapter 6: Shapeshifting

1. Ted Andrews, *Animal Speak* (Llewellyn Publications, 1996), p. 224.
2. Dorothy H. Eber, "Recording the Spirit World," *Natural History Magazine*, Sept, 2002, p. 54.
3. Don "Dream Seeker" Fasthorse, personal communication, March 14, 1992).
4. Andrews, *Animal Speak*, p. 224.
5. Michael Drake, *Power Animal Drumming: Calling the Spirits*. Talking Drum Publications, 2010. CD.
6. Thomas E. Mails, *Fools Crow: Wisdom and Power* (Council Oak Books, 2001) p 27.
7. Susan Grimaldi, "Tuvan Shamanism Comes to America." Shamanism (1998). Susan Grimaldi. Web. 28 Feb. 2012.
   <http://www.susangrimaldi.com/docs/tuvamerica.pdf>.
8. Susan Grimaldi, "Tuvan Shamanism Comes to America." Shamanism (1998). Susan Grimaldi. Web. 28 Feb. 2012.
   <http://www.susangrimaldi.com/docs/tuvamerica.pdf>.
9. Dhyani Ywahoo, *Voices of Our Ancestors: Cherokee Teachings from the Wisdom Fire* (Boston: Shambhala, 1987), p. 35.
10. Nicholas Noble Wolf. "Shamanic Drum and Shamanic Drumming." Nicholas Noble Wolf. Web. 9 Apr. 2012.
    <http://www.nicholasnoblewolf.com/q_and_a/drum_drumming.html>.
11. Samudranath, *Cities of Lightning: The Iconography of Thunder-Beings in the Oriental Traditions* (Blue Dolphin, 2000) p 12.

Chapter 7: Shamanic Music

1. Tim Hodgkinson, *Transcultural Collisions: Music and Shamanism in Siberia*. Tech. 11 Aug. 2008. Web. 28 Feb. 2012.
   <http://www.timhodgkinson.co.uk/transculturalcollisions.pdf>.
2. Kira Van Deusen, *Singing Story, Healing Drum: Shamans and Storytellers of Turkic Siberia* (McGill-Queen's Press, 2005), p 108.

3.	Ken Hyder, *Shamanism and Music in Siberia: Drum and Space*. Tech. 11 Aug. 2008. Web. 28 Feb. 2012. <http://www.soas.ac.uk/musicanddance/projects/project6/essays/file45912.pdf>.
4.	Gregory G. Maskarinec, *Rulings Of The Night: An Ethnography Of Nepalese Shaman Oral Texts*, (University of Wisconsin Press, 1995), p 187.
5.	Christina Pratt, *An Encyclopedia of Shamanism* (The Rosen Publishing Group, 2007), p. 128.
6.	Ken Hyder, *Shamanism and Music in Siberia: Drum and Space*. Tech. 11 Aug. 2008. Web. 28 Feb. 2012. <http://www.soas.ac.uk/musicanddance/projects/project6/essays/file45912.pdf>.
7.	Aaron Watson, 2001, "The Sounds of Transformation: Acoustics, Monuments and Ritual in the British Neolithic," In N. Price (ed.) *The Archaeology of Shamanism*. London: Routledge. 178-192.
8.	Beverley Diamond, *Visions of Sound: Musical Instruments of First Nations Communities in Northeastern America*, (University of Chicago Press, 1994), p. 90.
9.	Diamond, *Visions of Sound*, p. 87.
10.	Joseph Rael and Mary Marlow, *Being and Vibration* (Council Oak Books, 2002), p. 168.
11.	Guillermo Martinez, "Sounds of the Soul," *Sacred Hoop*, Issue 38, 2002, p. 8.

Chapter 8: Shamanic Drumming

1.	Kira Van Deusen, *Singing Story, Healing Drum: Shamans and Storytellers of Turkic Siberia* (McGill-Queen's Press, 2005), p. 122.
2.	Van Deusen, *Singing Story, Healing Drum*, p. 124.
3.	Mariko Namba Walter and Eva Jane Neumann Fridman, *Shamanism: An Encyclopedia of World Beliefs, Practices, and Culture* (ABC-CLIO, 2004), p. 95.
4.	Mihaly Csikszentmihalyi, *Flow: The Psychology of Optimal Experience* (New York: Harper & Row, 1990).
5.	Lisha Li. 1992. "The symbolization process of the shamanic drums used by the Manchus and other peoples in North Asia." *Yearbook for Traditional Music* 24:52-80.
6.	Dru Kristel, *Breath Was the First Drummer* (Santa Fe: QX Publications, 1997), p 87.
7.	Van Deusen, *Singing Story, Healing Drum*, p. 124.
8.	Michael Drake, *I Ching: The Tao of Drumming* (Talking Drum Publications, 2003).
9.	Christopher Forster and Tor Gjerde. *Sámi Mythology Shaman Drum*. Digital image. *Wikimedia Commons*. 31 May 2011. Web. 7 Mar. 2012. <http://commons.wikimedia.org/wiki/File:S%C3%A1mi_mythology_shaman_drum_Samisk_mytologi_schamantrumma_003.png>.
10.	Tor Gjerde, *Sámi Drums*. Tech. Web. 7 Mar. 2012. <http://old.no/samidrum/>.
11.	Richard Webster, *Oghams & Oracles: Divination in the Druidic Tradition* (Llewellyn Publications; 1st edition, 1995), p. 49.
12.	Patricia Peterson, "Shuunka Drumming Circle." *Hancock Parks District*. May 2010. Web. 28 Feb. 2012. http://www.hancockparks.com/TellUsYourStory/May2010Story.aspx>.

13. Theodore Craig Levin, Valentina Süzükei, *Where Rivers and Mountains Sing: Sound, Music, and Nomadism in Tuva and Beyond*, Volume 1 (Indiana University Press, 2006), p. 130

14. Levin, Süzükei, *Where Rivers and Mountains Sing*, p. 175.

15. Patricia Telesco, Don Two Eagles Waterhawk, *Sacred Beat: From the Heart of the Drum Circle*, (Red Wheel, 2003), p. 63.

16. Michael Drake, *Shamanic Journey Drumming*. Talking Drum Publications, 2008. CD.

17. Roger N. Walsh, Ph.D., *The Spirit Of Shamanism* (Jeremy P. Tarcher; 1990), p. 174.

Chapter 9: Shamanic Drumming Circles

1. Joseph Rael and Mary Marlow, *Being and Vibration* (Council Oak Books, 2002), p. 163.

2. Samudranath, *Cities of Lightning* (Blue Dolphin, 2000), p 12.

3. Michael Drake, *Thunder Beings Journey Drumming*. Talking Drum Publications, 2008. CD.

4. Barry Bittman, M.D., Karl T. Bruhn, Christine Stevens, MSW, MT-BC, James Westengard, Paul O Umbach, MA, "Recreational Music-Making...," *Advances in Mind-Body Medicine*, Fall/Winter 2003, Vol. 19 No. 3/4.

5. Michael Winkelman, *Shamanism: The Neural Ecology of Consciousness and Healing* (Westport, Conn: Bergin & Garvey; 2000), p. 148.

6. Barry Bittman, M.D., "Composite Effects of Group Drumming...," *Alternative Therapies in Health and Medicine*; Volume 7, No. 1, pp. 38-47; January 2001.

7. Robert Lawrence Friedman, *The Healing Power of the Drum* (Reno, NV: White Cliffs; 2000).

8. Edward Mikenas, "Drums, Not Drugs," *Percussive Notes*, April 1999:62-63.

9. Michael Winkelman, "Complementary Therapy for Addiction: Drumming Out Drugs," *American Journal of Public Health*; Apr 2003, Vol. 93 Issue 4, p647, 5p.

10. Joseph Rael and Mary Marlow, *Being and Vibration* (Council Oak Books, 2002), p. 163.

11. Mikenas, "Drums, Not Drugs," *Percussive Notes*; April 1999:62-63.

12. Friedman, *The Healing Power of the Drum*.

Afterword

1. Ed Buryn, *Vagabonding in the USA: A Guide for Independent Travelers and Foreign Visitors* (And/Or Press, 1980).

2. Dhyani Ywahoo, *Voices of Our Ancestors: Cherokee Teachings from the Wisdom Fire* (Boston: Shambhala, 1987), p. 16.

3. Michael Samuels and Mary Rockwood Lane, *Shaman Wisdom, Shaman Healing* (Wiley, 1st edition, 2003), p. 15.

4. Michael Winkelman, *Shamanism: The Neural Ecology of Consciousness and Healing* (Westport, Conn: Bergin & Garvey; 2000), p. 4.

About the Author

Michael Drake is an internationally respected writer and recording artist. He is the author of *The Shamanic Drum: A Guide to Sacred Drumming*, *I Ching: The Tao of Drumming*, and *Shamanic Drumming Circles Guide*. His musical albums include *Shamanic Journey Drumming*, *Power Animal Drumming*, and *Shaman's Drums*. His articles have appeared in numerous publications, including *Awareness*, *Sacred Hoop*, and *Mother Earth News*.

Raised in a conservative Baptist Church, Michael had his first ecstatic experience as a youth at a church revival, an evangelistic meeting intended to reawaken interest in religion. This state of rapture and trancelike elation inspired his spiritual quest for meaning and fulfillment. At a crucial point in his search, Michael came in touch with the transforming power of shamanic drumming and discovered his true calling. Inspired by his research and experiences, Michael founded Talking Drum Publications in 1991 in order to share the healing power of rhythm with the global drumming community. For the past twenty years he has been facilitating drum circles and hands-on experiential workshops nationwide. To learn more, visit Michael's website at http://ShamanicDrumming.com.